W9-ANJ-946

GREAT AUTHORS OF

CHILDREN'S
BOOKS

Essential Authors
for Children & Teens

GREAT AUTHORS OF

CHILDREN'S
BOOKS

EDITED BY JEANNE NAGLE

Britannica
Educational Publishing

IN ASSOCIATION WITH

ROSEN
EDUCATIONAL SERVICES

Published in 2014 by Britannica Educational Publishing (a trademark of Encyclopædia Britannica, Inc.) in association with The Rosen Publishing Group, Inc.

29 East 21st Street, New York, NY 10010

Copyright © 2014 The Rosen Publishing Group, Inc. and Encyclopædia Britannica, Inc.
Encyclopædia Britannica, Britannica, and the Thistle logo are registered trademarks of Encyclopædia Britannica, Inc. All rights reserved.

Distributed exclusively by Rosen Publishing.
To see additional Britannica Educational Publishing titles, go to rosenpublishing.com

First Edition

Britannica Educational Publishing
J.E. Luebering: Director, Core Reference Group
Anthony L. Green: Editor, Compton's by Britannica

Rosen Publishing
Hope Lourie Killcoyne: Executive Editor
Jeanne Nagle: Senior Editor
Nelson Sá: Art Director
Brian Garvey: Designer, Cover Design
Cindy Reiman: Photography Manager
Introduction by Laura Loria

Cataloging-in-Publication Data

Great authors of children's books/[editor] Jeanne Nagle.—First Edition.
    pages cm.—(Essential Authors for Children & Teens)
Includes bibliographical references and index.
ISBN 978-1-62275-096-2 (library binding)
1. Children's literature—Authorship—Juvenile literature. 2. Authors—Biography—Juvenile literature.
3. Young adult literature—Authorship—Juvenile literature. 4. Children—Books and reading—Juvenile
literature. I. Nagle, Jeanne, editor of compilation.
PN497.G74 2014
809'.89282—dc23
[B]
                                                                                          2013026994

Manufactured in the United States of America.

On the cover: Featured *(left to right)* are children's book authors Maurice Sendak, Judy Blume, and Ted Geisel, a.k.a. Dr. Seuss.

Cover, p. 3 aboikis/Shutterstock.com, cover, p.3 (inset, l to r) Theo Wargo/WireImage/Getty Images, Brad Camembert/Shutterstock.com, John Bryson/Time & Life Pictures/Getty Images; interior pages (books) © iStockphoto.com/AnthiaCumming, (colors) © iStockphoto.com/Phaucet

Contents

18

27

69

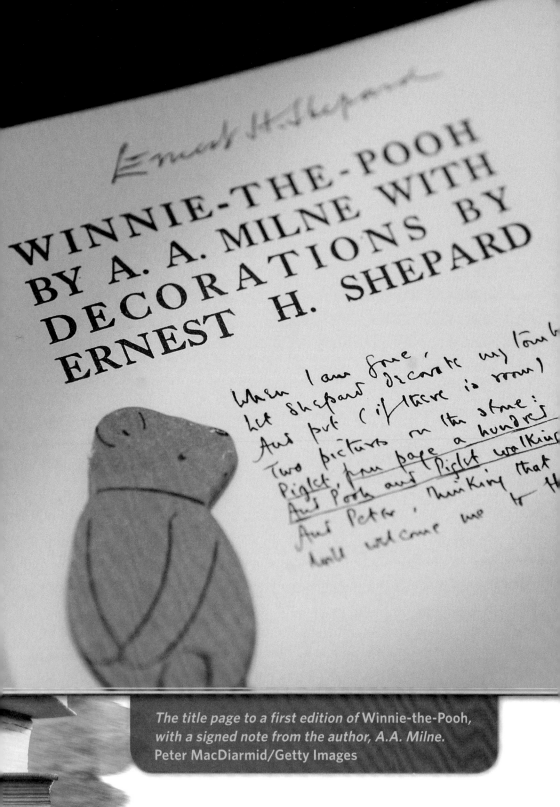

WINNIE-THE-POOH
BY A. A. MILNE WITH
DECORATIONS BY
ERNEST H. SHEPARD

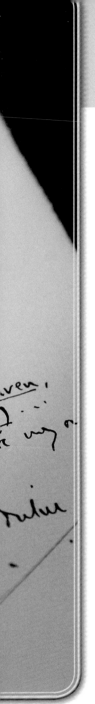

Introduction

The books that one reads at a young age leave an impression that lasts far beyond the final page. Children's books become part of a person, shaping his or her worldview well into adulthood. This book provides insight into the minds and lives of the people who have created some of the most influential and beloved children's books of all time.

Children's literature is a genre that encompasses a wide range of texts, from picture books to young-adult novels. For the youngest children, who are more often read to than read themselves, slim volumes with limited text and rich illustrations often become worn and frayed over repeated readings because they are so loved. Maurice Sendak, author of *Where the Wild Things Are* and many more stories, portrayed realistic, even naughty children in fantastical, slightly dark scenarios from which they return safely home in the end. Theodor Geisel, better known as Dr. Seuss, managed to turn an assignment to write a children's primer,

meaning a basic story for beginning readers, into the classic *The Cat in the Hat*.

Grade-schoolers move on to chapter books as their reading ability improves. Authors of chapter books at this level have the challenge of creating an engaging story while remaining conscious of their young readers' limited vocabulary and reference points. Beverly Cleary, a former children's librarian, created characters such as Ramona and Henry Huggins that appealed to children because of their ordinariness, as well as their tendency to get into humorous predicaments. Other authors take ordinary characters on extraordinary adventures. Welsh author Roald Dahl's *Charlie and the Chocolate Factory* and *James and the Giant Peach* were likely inspired by both his own childhood and his world travels as an adult. Stories about historical events or eras are also popular with the elementary set. Christopher Paul Curtis's *Bud, Not Buddy* and *The Watsons Go to Birmingham-1963* allow children to experience history through the eyes of a peer.

Middle-schoolers and teens are a challenging audience. Authors who write for

this age group must hold the readers' interest while not talking down to them. Judy Blume was a master at this. She revolutionized children's literature when she wrote about puberty, racism, and divorce in her novels, which include *Are You There God? It's Me, Margaret* and *Iggie's House*. Fantasy novels are also in demand at this age. J.R.R. Tolkien's tales of Middle Earth, *The Hobbit* and *The Lord of the Rings* series, were written between the 1930s and the 1950s but still command interest today. Adventurous readers enjoy the survivalist tales of Gary Paulsen, author of *Hatchet and Dogsong*. His life experiences as an Iditarod racer lend an authenticity to his stories.

The biographies in this book reveal how many children's book authors have had experiences similar to those faced by their characters. The bios also give readers a glimpse of how these folks came to be the authors of books that capture the imaginations of young readers and stir the hearts of those who have grown up but never outgrown certain texts.

RICHARD ADAMS

(b. 1920–)

English author Richard Adams was known for redefining anthropomorphic fiction, which gives human characteristics to animal characters. His most notable book was *Watership Down* (1972; film 1978), a novel that tell the story of a group of wild European rabbits seeking a new home after their warren is threatened by a housing development.

Richard George Adams was born on May 9, 1920, in Wash Common, Berkshire (now West Berkshire), Eng. Raised in a rural community outside Newbury, Berkshire, Adams led an isolated childhood mostly occupied by exploring his bucolic surroundings. He did not begin writing until 1966. While on a car trip with his daughters, he began telling them a story about a warren of rabbits; the girls urged him to put the story to paper. Adams penned the tale over the next two years, consulting a natural history study on rabbits to ensure that his main characters were depicted accurately. Unlike much anthropomorphic literature, the animal characters in *Watership Down*,

though able to talk, behave as they would in the wild.

The profits allowed Adams to begin writing full-time in 1974, producing several books for adults. He took a different approach to anthropomorphism with *Traveller* (1988), told from the perspective of Robert F. Lee's horse. He returned to his first book's familiar characters in 1996 with *Tales from Watership Down*, and his autobiography, *The Day Gone By*, was published in 1990.

Adams was president of the Royal Society for the Prevention of Cruelty to Animals (1980–82). He was inducted into the Royal Society of Literature in 1975.

AESOP

(d. 564? BCE)

What little is known of Aesop, the legendary Greek teller of fables, is recounted by such ancient Greek authors as Herodotus, Aristotle, Aristophanes, and Plutarch. Even from the mentions of him in this literature it is difficult to separate fact from fiction and to get a true picture of his life.

It seems generally agreed that Aesop was a native of Thrace, lived during the first half of the 6th century BCE, and spent part of his life as a slave on the island of Samos. The story in Plutarch's *Lives* that Aesop was a highly esteemed writer of fables living at the court of King Croesus of Lydia is probably

Aesop, with a fox, from the central medallion of a kylix, c. 470 BCE; in the Gregorian Etruscan Museum, Vatican City.Alinari/Art Resource, New York

untrue. That he was a writer of fables at all is unlikely, although he certainly gained a wide reputation in the ancient world as a teller of such stories.

Fables, or metaphorical animal stories, were often told to illustrate a point or teach a moral lesson, much as they are still told. Such was Aesop's reputation that most of the fables in ancient times were ascribed to him. They include such well-known stories as "The Shepherd Boy and the Wolf," "The Fox and the Grapes," and "The Hare and the Tortoise."

Modern editions of Aesop's fables are based on various ancient collections made by different authors from the 4th century BC to the 2nd century AD. Two of these collections are the anonymous *Augustana* and the compilation made by Babrius, a Greek writer of the 2nd century CE.

LOUISA MAY ALCOTT

(b. 1832–d. 1888)

Based on Louisa May Alcott's recollections of her own childhood, *Little*

Women describes the domestic adventures of a New England family of modest means but optimistic outlook. An immediate success when Alcott published it in 1868, the novel remains a classic of children's literature.

Louisa May Alcott was born in Germantown, Pa., on Nov. 29, 1832, and grew up in Boston and Concord, Mass. Her father, Amos Bronson Alcott, was a teacher and a transcendental philosopher, a close friend of Ralph Waldo Emerson's. Alcott's "conversational" method of teaching was far in advance of his time and won him few pupils. It was, however, very successful with Louisa. She began to write poems and stories, and by age 15 she was writing and producing amateur theatricals. She published some of her stories under the name A.M. Barnard; these lurid and violent thrillers were unusual in their depictions of women as strong, self-reliant, and imaginative. By 1860 her verses and stories were appearing in *The Atlantic Monthly*.

In 1862, during the Civil War, Louisa Alcott served as a nurse in the Union hospital at Georgetown, now part of Washington, D.C. She contracted typhoid from unsanitary conditions and was sent home. She was

Louisa May Alcott. Courtesy of Louisa May Alcott Memorial Association

never completely well again. Her letters home telling of her hospital experiences were published in 1863 under the title *Hospital Sketches* and brought her $2,000. With this money she made her first trip to Europe.

On her return she began *Little Women*, a realistic but wholesome picture of family life with which younger readers could easily identify. The book made her famous and enabled her to pay off all the family debts. In 1870 Alcott took a long tour of Europe with her sister May. In Rome she wrote *Little Men* (1871).

Alcott's other works include *An Old-Fashioned Girl* (1870), *Eight Cousins* (1875), *Under the Lilacs* (1878), and *Jo's Boys* (1886). The publication of some of her lesser-known works late in the 20th century aroused renewed critical interest in her adult fiction, such as the Gothic novels *A Modern Mephistopheles* (1877; republished 1987) and *A Long Fatal Love Chase* (first published 1995).

Alcott took an active part in the temperance and the woman's suffrage movements. She never married. She died in Boston on March 6, 1888, two days after her father.

Orchard House, in Concord, where she wrote *Little Women*, was made a memorial in 1911.

HANS CHRISTIAN ANDERSEN

(b. 1805–d. 1875)

A native of Denmark, Hans Christian Andersen is one of the immortals of world literature. The fairy tales he wrote are like no others written before or since.

Andersen was born in Odense, a village on the Danish island of Fyn, on April 2, 1805. During the early years of his childhood his grandmother told him old Danish folk tales and legends, and he acted out plays in a homemade puppet theater. As a young boy, he went to school only at intervals, spending most of his time imagining stories rather than reading lessons.

Andersen was apprenticed first to a weaver, then to a tobacconist, and finally to a tailor. Yet he knew these occupations were not for him. The only things that held

his interest were the theater, books, and stories. When he was 14, he decided to go to Copenhagen, the capital of Denmark, and seek his fortune. There followed three bitter years of poverty as Andersen tried his hand at singing, dancing, and acting

At last, when he was 17, Andersen came to the attention of Chancellor Jonas Collin, a director of the Royal Theater. Collin had read a play by Andersen and saw that the youth had talent, though he lacked education. Collin arranged for him to study under a private tutor in Copenhagen. In 1828, when he was 23, Andersen passed his entrance examinations to the university in Copenhagen.

Andersen's writings began to be published in Danish in 1829. His first works were poems, plays, novels, and impressions of his travels. In 1835 he published four short stories under the collected title *Tales, Told for Children*. Two further installments of stories were added to make up a fuller first volume of the book, published in 1837; a second volume was completed in 1842.

Over the course of his lifetime, Andersen published 168 fairy tales in all. Some of his most well-known stories include "The Snow Queen," "The Princess and the Pea," and

"The Little Mermaid." Andersen died in Copenhagen on Aug. 4, 1875.

L. FRANK BAUM

(b. 1856–d. 1919)

The Wonderful Wizard of Oz made L. Frank Baum famous as an author of children's literature. By the 1970s it had become one of the 15 best-selling books of the 20th century.

Lyman Frank Baum was born in Chittenango, N.Y., on May 15, 1856. He attended school in Syracuse, N.Y., and showed an early interest in writing. He worked as a newspaper editor in Aberdeen, S.D., from 1888 to 1890 and in Chicago, Ill., from 1897 to 1902.

Baum's first children's book, *Father Goose*, was an instant success when it was published in 1899. Other popular works were *The Life and Adventures of Santa Claus*, *The Enchanted Isle of Yew*, and *Sky Island*. In all, Baum wrote about 60 books, many under pen names.

A modern fairy tale, *The Wonderful Wizard of Oz* tells the story of Dorothy, a

L. Frank Baum. © AP Images

Kansas farm girl who is blown by a cyclone to the imaginary land of Oz. First produced as a stage musical in 1902, *The Wizard* appeared in film form in 1925; a later version in 1939 became a movie classic, released as *The Wonderful Wizard of Oz*. A black contemporary adaptation called *The Wiz* opened as a Broadway musical in 1975; a motion picture version was released in 1978.

The Wonderful Wizard of Oz was followed by 13 other Oz books. Other writers continued the Oz series after Baum's death in Hollywood, Calif., on May 6, 1919.

JUDY BLUME

(b. 1938–)

As a youth, U.S. author Judy Blume was discouraged by encountering a lack of books with characters whose feelings and actions resembled her own. She attempted to rectify this as an adult by creating juvenile fiction with people and situations identifiable to young readers. While her frankness, first-person narratives, and ability to portray the concerns of her audience with humor made her a remarkably popular

and award-winning author, her works often were banned because of objections to her subject matter and language.

Blume was born Judy Sussman on Feb. 12, 1938, in Elizabeth, N.J. After graduating from high school with high honors, she attended New York University and received a bachelor's degree in education in 1960. In 1959 she married John Blume, with whom she had two children. The couple divorced in the 1970s.

While enrolled in a continuing education course on writing for children and teenagers, Blume produced a draft of what became her first published book, *The One in the Middle Is the Green Kangaroo* (1969). At about the same time she published a version of a later book, *Iggie's House* in *Trailblazer* magazine; she rewrote it for publication by Bradbury Press in 1970.

Blume made a huge splash in the world of children's literature with the publication of *Are You There God? It's Me, Margaret* in 1970, a preteen novel based on her own memories of adolescence. Many critics praised her willingness to tackle puberty and other sensitive subject matter in an honest, understandable way, and the *New York Times* ranked the book among the

year's best. Many young readers wrote letters to tell Blume that they identified with Margaret and her dilemmas. Some adults, however, deemed the book inappropriate and wanted it removed from library shelves.

Blume solidified her standing as a leading author of books for young adults with novels such as *Then Again, Maybe I Won't* (1971), *It's Not the End of the World* (1972), *Deenie* (1973), *Tiger Eyes* (1981), *Just as Long as We're Together* (1987), and *Here's to You, Rachel Robinson* (1993). Issues of censorship, however, continued to surround her work, especially *Forever* (1975), a story about a young couple experiencing love and sex for the first time.

Blume wrote several books for middle-school readers, including *Tales of a Fourth Grade Nothing* (1972), *Otherwise Known as Sheila the Great* (1972), *Blubber* (1974), *Superfudge* (1980), and *Fudge-a-Mania* (1990). Like her books for older audiences, they contained language, situations, and concerns that rang true to the age group. The humorous Fudge books served as the basis for a Saturday morning television show that premiered in 1995.

Blume also penned two novels for adults, *Wifey* (1978) and *Smart Women* (1983). She

Judy Blume, signing books at the 2012 Los Angeles Times Festival of Books. David Livingston/Getty Images

collected letters from young readers for the book *Letters to Judy: What Your Kids Wish They Could Tell You* (1986). Proceeds from that book and select others went to the KIDS Fund, which she established in 1981 to offer support to nonprofit organizations that encouraged communication between parents and children.

Among Blume's many honors were the Eleanor Roosevelt Humanitarian Award (1983), the Carl Sandburg Freedom to Read Award (1984), and the Big Brothers/Big Sisters National Hero Award (1992). She also was recognized by the American Civil Liberties Union and in countless readers' choice surveys.

EVE BUNTING

(b. 1928–)

U.S. author Eve Bunting produced more than 150 publications for juvenile audiences, ranging from picture books to middle-grade stories to young-adult novels. The Catholic Library Association recognized her extensive contributions to children's literature by awarding her the 1997 Regina Medal.

She was born Anne Evelyn Bolton on Dec. 19, 1928, in Maghera, Northern Ireland. Following study at Methodist College and Queen's University in Belfast during the 1930s and 1940s, she married Edward Davison Bunting in 1951. The couple and their three children moved to the United States around 1960 and settled in California.

An adult-education course on writing for publication taken at Pasadena City College inspired Bunting to pursue a career as an author. Her first published book, *The Two Giants* (1972), retold a traditional Irish tale. She went on to work in various genres, including science fiction, romances, mysteries, animal nonfiction, and contemporary fiction. Some of her works appeared under the names Evelyn Bolton or A.E. Bunting.

The Los Angeles riots of 1992 prompted Bunting to write *Smoky Night* (1994), a picture book about a child witnessing urban rioting in his own neighborhood. David

Diaz received the 1995 Caldecott Medal for his illustration of the book. Many of her other picture books also presented serious themes not often covered in publications for young readers. *The Wall* (1990) conveyed the significance of the Vietnam Memorial, while *Fly Away Home* (1991) dealt with homelessness.

Some of Bunting's best-known books for middle-school and young-adult readers featured realistic plots and showed the growth of characters who faced challenging situations. The subjects that she explored included suicide.

Bunting's work was honored by organizations such as the Child Study Association of America, the *New York Times*, *School Library Journal*, the Parents' Choice Foundation, and the Southern California Council on Literature for Children and Young People. She received back-to-back Golden Kite Awards from the Society of Children's Book Writers for *One More Flight* (1976) and *Ghost of Summer* (1977). *Coffin on a Case* (1992) won an Edgar Award as the year's best juvenile mystery.

Bunting taught writing at the University of California, Los Angeles, and at various writers' conferences. She discussed her life and work in *Once Upon a Time* (1995).

FRANCES HODGSON BURNETT

(b. 1849–d. 1924)

B ritish-born U.S. author Frances Hodgson Burnett wrote many novels and stories for adults and children, as well as several plays. Her most famous work is *Little Lord Fauntleroy*, a story about a young American boy who becomes heir to an English earldom.

Frances Hodgson was born on Nov. 24, 1849, in Manchester, England. She grew up in increasingly poor circumstances after the death of her father in 1854. In 1865 the family immigrated to the United States and settled in New Market, near Knoxville, Tenn., where the promise of support from a maternal uncle failed to materialize.

In 1868 Hodgson managed to place a story with the journal *Godey's Lady's Book.* Within a few years she was being published regularly in *Godey's, Peterson's Ladies' Magazine, Scribner's Monthly,* and *Harper's.* In 1873, after a year's visit to England, she married Dr. Swan Moses Burnett of New Market (they were divorced in 1898).

Burnett's first novel, *That Lass o' Lowrie's,* which had been serialized in *Scribner's,* was published in 1877. After moving with her husband to Washington, D.C., Burnett wrote the novels *Haworth's* (1879), *Louisiana* (1880), *A Fair Barbarian* (1881), and *Through One Administration* (1883), as well as a play, *Esmeralda* (1881), written with actor-playwright William Gillette.

In 1886 Burnett's most famous and successful book appeared. First serialized in *St. Nicholas* magazine, *Little Lord Fauntleroy* was intended as a children's book, but it had its greatest appeal to mothers. The title character was described as being dressed lavishly in black velvet, lace collar, and long golden curls. The story became so popular that the term "Little Lord Fauntleroy" has come to mean a type of children's clothing—or a pampered, effeminate little boy. The book sold more than half a million copies, and

Frances Hodgson Burnett.

Burnett's income was increased by her dramatized version, which quickly became a repertory standard.

Burnett's later books include *Sara Crewe* (1888), dramatized as *The Little Princess* (1905), and *The Secret Garden* (1909), both of which were also written for children. The latter book, considered Burnett's best, has become a classic of children's literature. *The Lady of Quality* (1896) has been considered the best of her other plays. In 1893 she published a memoir of her youth, *The One I Knew Best of All*.

From the mid-1890s she lived mainly in England, but in 1909 she built a house in Plandome, Long Island, N.Y., where she died on Oct. 29, 1924. Her son Vivian Burnett, the model for Little Lord Fauntleroy, wrote a biography of her in 1927 entitled *The Romantick Lady*.

LEWIS CARROLL

(b. 1832–d. 1898)

British author, mathematician, and logician Charles Dodgson, best known by his pen name of Lewis Carroll, is renowned

for writing two of the most famous and admired children's books in the world, *Alice's Adventures in Wonderland* and its sequel, *Through the Looking-Glass*. He also wrote poetry for children, including the famous nonsense poem *The Hunting of the Snark*.

Charles Lutwidge Dodgson was born on Jan. 27, 1832, at Daresbury in Cheshire, England. His father was a clergyman. Charles was the eldest of 11 children—four boys and seven girls. When he was 12 years old, he was sent to school at nearby Rutland, and two years later he entered Rugby. There he earned good grades in classical languages and mathematics.

When he was 18, Charles entered Christ Church College, Oxford University, where he studied, worked, and lived for the rest of his life. There he took his bachelor's and master's degrees, was ordained a deacon of the Church of England, and taught mathematics to several generations of Oxford students. A shy man who suffered from a bad stammer, he never married. His few adult friends were mainly fellow faculty members. His hobbies were mathematical puzzles and photography.

Dodgson always loved children. In his youth, he had spent much of his time

inventing games to play with his younger brothers and sisters. As an adult, he often gave parties for children and took them to the theater and on picnics. On one such picnic his guests were Alice, Lorina, and Edith, the daughters of Dr. Henry Liddell, dean of Christ Church College. On this hot summer day in a meadow along the Isis River he began to tell them the "Alice" stories. Later he wrote them out for the children, and the manuscript tales were read and reread by many people. *Alice's Adventures in Wonderland* was published in 1864, and *Through the Looking-Glass* appeared in 1871. Both were illustrated by the famous cartoonist and artist Sir John Tenniel. Both were also published under Dodgson's pen name, which he created by translating his first and middle names, Charles and Lutwidge, into Latin as Carolus Ludovicus, and then reversing and retranslating them into English.

In 1876 he published *The Hunting of the Snark*, the amusing subtitle of which is *An Agony in Eight Fits*. Other important children's books written by him were *Sylvie and Bruno* (1889) and *Sylvie and Bruno Concluded* (1893). To these books he signed his pen name; for several other works on

Alice in Wonderland *author Lewis Caroll.* Gabriel Benzur/
Time & Life Pictures/Getty Images

mathematics and logic he used his real name. His book royalties enabled him to teach fewer classes, and he spent his summers at Eastbourne on the seacoast. He died on Jan. 14, 1898.

BEVERLY CLEARY

(b. 1916–)

The books of U.S. children's author Beverly Cleary won many awards and captured the imagination. Her strong following of young readers was drawn by the kind of stories that the author had wanted to read as a child but could never find.

She was born Beverly Bunn on April 12, 1916, in McMinnville, Ore. She received a B.A. degree from the University of California at Berkeley in 1938 and a B.A. in librarianship in 1939 from the University of Washington in Seattle. She worked as a children's librarian in Yakima, Wash., from 1939 to 1940, and as a post librarian from 1943 to 1945 at the U.S. Army Hospital in Oakland, Calif.

Cleary wrote amusing tales about memorable characters. Her first book

Beverly Cleary, standing in the doorway of a toy shop in the 1980s. Terry Smith/Time & Life Pictures/Getty Images

introduced readers to *Henry Huggins* (1950), who became the main character in a number of Cleary's works. She also produced a series of books starring Ramona Quimby, an independent-minded youngster and the Ramona series, whose adventures are both humorous and realistic. Notable titles in the series include *Ramona the Pest* (1968),

Ramona and Her Father (1977), and *Ramona Quimby, Age 8* (1981). Among Cleary's other books were *Ellen Tebbits* (1951), *Otis Spofford* (1953), *The Luckiest Girl* (1958), *The Real Hole* (1960), *The Mouse and the Motorcycle* (1965), *Runaway Ralph* (1970), and *Dear Mr. Henshaw* (1983).

Cleary received the Laura Ingalls Wilder Award from the American Library Association in 1975 for her lasting contribution to children's literature. The same year she was awarded a Distinguished Alumna Award from the University of Washington. She won the Newbery Honor Book Award in 1978 for *Ramona and her Father*. In 1980 she was awarded the Catholic Library Assocation's Regina Medal for her contributions to children's literature.

SHARON CREECH

(b. 1945–)

The American Library Association awarded U.S. author Sharon Creech the 1995 Newbery Medal for *Walk Two Moons* (1994), her first book published in the United States. She was a runner-up for the prestigious honor again in 2001 for *The Wanderer* (2000).

Sharon Creech was born on July 29, 1945, in Cleveland, Ohio. She enjoyed writing and reading as a youth and especially liked mythology. After receiving a bachelor's degree from Hiram College in Ohio, she moved to Washington, D.C., to attend George Mason University in nearby Fairfax, Va. Creech moved to Thorpe, Surrey, England, in 1979 to teach English at a campus of The American School in Switzerland (TASIS), a boarding school.

While continuing to teach American and British literature to teenagers, Creech worked on her own writing. She published the adult novels *The Recital* (1990) and *Nickel Malley* (1991) under the name Sharon Rigg. Her first children's book, *Absolutely Normal Chaos*, debuted in England in 1990. She styled the book as the journal of a 13-year-old girl telling of the people and events that comprise her summer

Creech was virtually unknown in the United States until the release of *Walk Two Moons*, which, in addition to winning the Newbery Medal, was named one of the best books of 1994 by *School Library Journal*. A story about a teenage girl traveling to Idaho

with her grandparents to visit her mother, it was inspired by a car trip Creech took with her family during her youth.

Creech followed up *Walk Two Moons* with *Pleasing the Ghost* (1996), *Chasing Redbird* (1997),and *The Wanderer*, which was a runner-up for the Newbery Medal in 2001. She also wrote short stories and poetry.

CHRISTOPHER PAUL CURTIS

(b. 1953–)

The novel *Bud, Not Buddy* (1999) earned U.S. author Christopher Paul Curtis both the 2000 Newbery Medal and the Coretta Scott King Author award. Curtis was the first writer to win both prestigious children's literature prizes in the same year.

Curtis was born on May 10, 1953, in Flint, Mich. After high school he worked at an auto plant for 13 years. Writing in a journal on his breaks helped Curtis deal with the monotony of the automobile assembly line. He later took classes part-time at the

University of Michigan's Flint campus, earning his bachelor's degree in political science in 1996.

With the support of his wife and children, Curtis took a year off work to concentrate on writing. A manuscript he entered in a national contest impressed an editor from Delacorte Press, resulting in his first publication, *The Watsons Go to Birmingham—1963* (1995). The story of an African American family from Michigan that travels to the South to visit relatives in the summer of 1963, Curtis drew some of the inspiration from his own childhood and spent a great deal of time doing research in order to ensure historical accuracy. The publication was chosen as an honor book for both the Newbery and Coretta Scott King prizes, making it one of the most successful debut novels in the history of children's literature. Like his next work, *Bud, Not Buddy*—the story of an orphaned 10-year-old who runs away from a bad foster home during the Great Depression to search for his father—critics praised the book for its ability to appeal to readers of all ages and races, its interesting treatment of serious subject matter, and its entertaining characters.

Curtis's creative output continued into the 21st century. The modern-day fairy tale *Bucking the Sarge* (2004) is narrated by a teenaged boy whose mother, a selfish slumlord, is called "the Sarge." *Mr. Chickee's Funny Money* (2005) details the adventures of an overachieving seven-year-old who aspires to become a detective. Curtis's next book, *Elijah of Buxton* (2007), follows a young slave who faces danger after escaping to Canada on the Underground Railroad. The *Mighty Miss Malone* (2012) is set during the Depression and centers on a 12-year-old girl who first appeared in *Bud, Not Buddy*.

ROALD DAHL

(b. 1916–d. 1990)

Although British author Roald Dahl wrote many books for adults, he is best known for his action-packed children's books filled with memorable, magical, and often bizarre characters. Many of his works feature children triumphing over cruel and beastly adults.

Dahl was born on Sept. 13, 1916, in Llandaff, Glamorgan, Wales. His family moved to Kent, England, after his father died in 1920. After graduating from high school, he worked for Shell Oil Company in London and then Dar es Salaam, Tanzania. From 1939 to 1945, Dahl served in the Royal Air Force, and injuries he received while

Author Roald Dahl, reading to his children at home in Buckinghamshire, England, in 1965. Leonard McCombe/ Time & Life Pictures/Getty Images

flying as a fighter pilot plagued him for the rest of his life. His stories about the military were published in popular magazines and in the book *Over to You* (1946). His first children's book, *The Gremlins* (1943), told of mean little creatures who make fighter aircraft crash. During the 1950s he concentrated on writing horror stories for adults.

Dahl's interest in juvenile literature resurfaced when he began making up bedtime stories for his own children. One of his earliest successes was *Charlie and the Chocolate Factory* (1964), a story about a poor boy whose luck changes when he gets to visit the workshop of Willy Wonka, a charismatic candy maker. Dahl later turned the novel into the screenplay for the film *Willy Wonka and the Chocolate Factory* (1971). Some of his other screenwriting credits include *You Only Live Twice* (1967) and *Chitty Chitty Bang Bang* (1968), both based on novels by Ian Fleming. Dahl's own books *James and the Giant Peach* (1961), *The Witches* (1983), and *Matilda* (1988) were adapted by others into movies during the 1990s. He also wrote two autobiographies, *Boy: Tales of Childhood* (1984) and *Going Solo* (1986). Dahl died in Oxford, England, on Nov. 23, 1990.

MARGUERITE LOFFT DE ANGELI

(b. 1889–d. 1987)

U.S. author Marguerite Lofft De Angeli's characters came from a variety of backgrounds, time periods, and places. Through these characters, readers could recognize experiences and concerns similar to their own.

Born on March 14, 1889, in Lapeer, Mich., De Angeli enjoyed reading and drawing during her youth, and as a teenager she focused on developing her singing talent and performed locally. She studied drawing under the guidance of illustrator Maurice Bower while her children were young, and her work steadily appeared in magazines and books starting in 1922. During her career she provided illustrations to accompany the text of such notable authors as Cornelia Meigs, Elizabeth Gray Vining, Eric Kelly, and Elizabeth Coatsworth.

With the encouragement of a publishing company, De Angeli began writing her own books. Her first, *Ted and Nina Go to the Grocery Store* (1935), was based on

experiences of her own children. Its success led to *Ted and Nina Have a Happy Rainy Day* (1936) and *A Summer Day with Ted and Nina* (1940).

De Angeli won the Newbery Medal in 1950 for *The Door in the Wall* (1949), a piece of historical fiction about a crippled British boy who finds a way to help save his medieval city. *Black Fox of Lorne* (1956) was selected as a 1957 Newbery Honor Book; it tells of twins shipwrecked off the coast of medieval Scotland whose cleverness keeps them alive and enables them to avenge their father's murder. Also highly regarded for her illustrations, De Angeli twice was a runner-up for the Caldecott Medal

De Angeli's other self-illustrated books include *Henner's Lydia* (1936), *Copper-Toed Boots* (1938), *Thee, Hannah!* (1940), and *Jared's Island* (1947). *Bright April* (1946) was one of the first modern children's books to deal with an African American child encountering racial prejudice.

In 1971 De Angeli published the autobiography *Butter at the Old Price*. She created her last book, *Friendship and Other Poems* (1981), when she was 92 years old. De Angeli died on June 16, 1987, in Philadelphia, Pa.

MEINDERT DE JONG

(b. 1906–d. 1991)

For his contributions to children's literature, U.S. author Meindert De Jong earned the Hans Christian Andersen International Children's Book Medal in 1962 and the Catholic Library Association's Regina Medal in 1972. In 1969 his *Journey from Peppermint Street* won the first National Book Award for children's literature. Like many of De Jong's books, the story was set in his native Holland.

De Jong was born on March 4, 1906, in Wierum, The Netherlands. His family moved to the United States when he was eight, and the prejudices they faced as newcomers later influenced his writing. He took on various jobs after graduating from Calvin College in Michigan in 1928. While working as a poultry farmer in Iowa, he told stories about his animals. A local librarian suggested that he turn his tales into a children's book, and he created *The Big Goose and the Little White Duck* (1938). Its popularity led him to abandon farming for a writing career, and he worked for the Federal Writers'

Project in Michigan while establishing himself as a children's author.

De Jong enjoyed enormous success during the 1950s. In 1954 both *Hurry Home, Candy* (1953) and *Shadrach* (1953) were chosen by the American Library Association as Newbery Honor Books. The two books, the former about a stray dog looking for a home and the latter about a boy's love for his pet rabbit, were among the many De Jong wrote about animals. Like many other publications to come, they were enhanced with illustrations by Maurice Sendak. De Jong received the 1955 Newbery Medal for *The Wheel on the School* (1954), a story about a Dutch community coming together to help schoolchildren with their wish to attract storks back to the village. He was a runner-up for the award in 1957 with *The House of Sixty Fathers* (1956), which was inspired by a friendship he had with a Chinese boy while serving in World War II. *Along Came a Dog* (1958), a 1959 Newbery Honor Book, was one of De Jong's many publications to focus sensitively on the plight of misfits.

De Jong's other publications include *Bells of the Harbor* (1941), *Billy and the Unhappy Bull* (1946), *The Tower by the Sea* (1950), *Far Out the Long Canal* (1964), and *The Easter Cat* (1971). His works were translated into

many languages and published throughout the world. De Jong died on July 16, 1991, in Allegan, Mich.

KATE DICAMILLO

(b. 1964–)

Best-selling U.S. author and screenwriter Kate DiCamillo was known for her delicate and effective treatment of difficult topics such as death, separation, and loss. Only four years after she published her first novel, DiCamillo was awarded the Newbery Medal for her book *The Tale of Despereaux* (2003).

Katrina Elizabeth DiCamillo was born on March 25, 1964, in Philadelphia, Penn. She was frequently sick and hospitalized with pneumonia in her youth. Since she could not physically escape her room, DiCamillo used her imagination to entertain herself and change her circumstances. This skill was most useful in her writing. In 1987 she graduated from the University of Florida at Gainesville with a bachelor's degree in English.

After pursuing various short-term jobs, DiCamillo moved to Minneapolis, Minn.,

Kate DiCamillo. Gregg DeGuire/WireImage/Getty Images

where she worked in a book warehouse and developed an interest in writing children's literature. Her first novel, *Because of Winn-Dixie* (2000; film 2005), features 10-year-old Opal, who learns acceptance and friendship with help from Winn-Dixie, her friendly dog. *Because of Winn-Dixie* won a Newbery Honor in 2001.

The Tale of Despereaux: Being the Story of a Mouse, a Princess, Some Soup, and a Spool of Thread (2003; film 2008) is a story about four outcasts, including the main character, a mouse named Despereaux Tilling. DiCamillo explored the themes of love and forgiveness through the isolation these characters face. In 2004 *The Tale of Despereaux* won the Newbery Award.

DiCamillo went on to publish a series of chapter books about Mercy Watson, a pig that loves toast, including *Mercy Watson to the Rescue* (2005) and *Mercy Watson: Princess in Disguise* (2007). Another novel, *The Miraculous Journey of Edward Tulane* (2006), tells the story of a rabbit that learns how to love, while *The Magician's Elephant* (2009) details the mysterious events that connect a magician, an orphan, and an elephant.

ELEANOR ESTES

(b. 1906–d. 1988)

During a career spanning almost half a century, U.S. author Eleanor Estes penned some 15 juvenile books. Her ability to write about events through the eyes of a child brought her popular and critical success.

She was born Eleanor Ruth Rosenfeld on May 9, 1906, in West Haven, Conn. After graduating from high school in 1923, she took a job at the New Haven Public Library and later earned a scholarship to the Pratt Institute Library School. She met Rice Estes while at Pratt, and they married in December 1932. For the remainder of the decade, she was a children's librarian at branches of the New York Public Library.

Eleanor Estes published her first book, *The Moffats*, in 1941. In simple but authentic prose, it chronicled the everyday adventures of a poor but happy small-town New England family during the World War I era. Estes continued to write about the four Moffat children and their widowed mother in *The Middle Moffat* (1942) and *Rufus M.* (1943), both of which were selected by the American Library Association as Newbery Honor Books. Forty years later, Estes delighted fans by creating another sequel, *The Moffat Museum* (1983).

Estes won the Newbery Medal in 1952 for *Ginger Pye* (1951), a self-illustrated book about a brother and sister searching for their lost puppy. The Pye family adopts a black kitten with unusual abilities in the sequel *Pinky Pye* (1958).

Another of Estes's well-known publications is the 1945 Newbery Honor Book *The Hundred Dresses* (1944), a story about an immigrant girl who gets teased by classmates. Estes often mixed fantasy and reality, as in the books *The Witch Family* (1960) and *The Curious Adventures of Jimmy McGee* (1987). Her other works include *The Alley* (1964), *The Tunnel of Hugsy Goode* (1972), and *The Lost Umbrella of Kim Chu* (1978). She also wrote an adult novel, *The Echoing Green* (1947). Estes died on July 15, 1988, in Hamden, Conn., of complications following a stroke.

PAUL FLEISCHMAN

(b. 1952–)

Paying close attention to both the sound of his writing and the sounds within the story, Paul Fleischman created novels, poems, short stories, and picture books that come alive for young readers.

Fleischman was born on Sept. 5, 1952, in Monterey, Calif. The son of prominent children's author Sid Fleischman, he grew up listening to drafts of his father's books. He attended the University of California at Berkeley in the early 1970s and earned a bachelor's degree from the University of New Mexico in 1977.

Fleischman published his first book, *The Birthday Tree*, in 1979. His second effort, *The Half-a-Moon Inn* (1980), was his first work chosen by the Society of Children's Book Writers as a Golden Kite Honor Book. In 1983 his book of short stories *Graven Images* (1982) was selected as a Newbery Honor Book, while the Parents' Choice Foundation honored *Path of the Pale Horse* (1983).

Fleischman received the 1989 Newbery Medal for *Joyful Noise: Poems for Two Voices* (1988). Each of the 14 poems in the collection focuses on a different insect. Although Fleischman gives each creature a personality, the characters remain true to nature concerning such things as life cycle and habits, thus informing readers about the insect world as well as entertaining them. As the title suggests, the poems were designed to be read aloud by alternating readers. Fleischman published *I Am Phoenix: Poems for Two Voices*, a similar book, this time about birds, in 1985. He also wrote *Townsend's Warbler* (1992), a nonfiction book about John Rowe Townsend's discovery of a new bird species.

Like his father, Fleischman gave many of his books historical settings. The tales in *Coming-and-Going Men* (1985) feature details and language true to Vermont in the 1800s, while *Bull Run* (1993) tells the stories of individuals participating in the Battle of Bull Run during the American Civil War. *Dateline: Troy* (1996) places newspaper collages alongside text about the Trojan War to show readers the modern equivalents of the events.

ESTHER FORBES

(b. 1891–d. 1967)

E sther Forbes's historical works, both fiction and nonfiction, brought the lives of young people in early America to life for contemporary readers. Young readers know her best for her novel *Johnny Tremaine*.

Esther Louise Forbes was born on June 28, 1891, in Westborough, Mass. She studied at Bradford Junior College and the University of Wisconsin. She later served on the staff of Houghton Mifflin publishers in Boston from 1920 to 1926 and from 1942 to 1946.

Forbes received the Pulitzer Prize in history in 1943 for *Paul Revere and the World He Lived In* (1942). The book examines Revere both as an artisan and as a member of the New England community that was pivotal at the time of the American Revolution. Her other historical studies included *A Mirror for Witches* (1928) and *America's Paul Revere* (1946).

Johnny Tremain: A Novel for Young and Old (1943), which won the 1944 Newbery

Medal, was Forbes's only novel written for children. It became a favorite of students, teachers, and curious readers of all ages. The novel, which traces the development of a young orphan boy from his days as a silversmith's apprentice to his participation in the American Revolution, evolved from the author's research for her book on Paul Revere. It was made into a motion picture by Walt Disney and into a television show.

Forbes's novels for adults included *Paradise* (1937), *The Running of the Tide* (1948), and *Rainbow on the Road* (1959). *The Running of the Tide*, which was set in Salem, Mass., before the War of 1812, was made into a motion picture after having won the Metro-Goldwyn-Mayer novel award.

Forbes's novels were also translated into more than 10 languages. The author was awarded honorary degrees from Clark University, the University of Maine, the University of Wisconsin, Northeastern University, Wellesley College, and Tufts University. She died on Aug. 12, 1967, in Worcester, Mass.

DON FREEMAN

(b. 1908–d. 1978)

U.S. author and illustrator Don Freeman created more than 30 children's books characterized by humor, readability, and sincerity. Many of his stories center on animal characters.

Freeman was born on Aug. 11, 1908, in San Diego, Calif. He moved to New York City in the late 1920s to work as a musician and to study at the Art Students League. He later became a freelance graphic artist and sketched for the drama sections of the *New York Times*, the *Herald Tribune*, and other publications. Some of his artwork on theatrical themes was later exhibited at the National Museum of American Art in Washington, D.C.

Freeman began writing and illustrating children's books in the 1950s. He is perhaps best known for creating the character Corduroy, a teddy bear featured in *Corduroy* (1968) and *A Pocket for Corduroy* (1978). Among his other children's books are *Mop Top* (1955), *Norman the Doorman* (1959), *Dandelion* (1964), *Inspector Peckit* (1972), and *Bearymore* (1976). *Pet of the*

Met (1953)—a collaboration with his wife, Lydia—received a *Herald Tribune* Spring Festival award.

In addition to creating his own books, Freeman illustrated a number of works by other authors, including William Saroyan's *My Name Is Aram* (1940) and *The Human Comedy* (1943) and James Thurber's *The White Deer* (1945). He also wrote *It Shouldn't Happen* (1945) and the autobiography *Come One, Come All!* (1949) for adult audiences. He died on Feb. 1, 1978, in New York City. After his death, various authors wrote books featuring his popular Corduroy character.

NEIL GAIMAN

(b. 1960–)

British writer Neil Gaiman published numerous science fiction and fantasy novels, graphic novels, and comics. But Gaiman is also the author of children's books, including the Newbery Medal-winning *The Graveyard Book* (2008).

Born on Nov. 10, 1960, Neil Richard Gaiman was a graduate of Whitgift School

in Croydon. A career in journalism preceded his breakthrough as a writer of notion and fiction books for adults. It wasn't until 2002 that Gaiman achieved fame as a writer of children's literature. That was the year he published *Coraline*, which won the Hugo Award for best novella and was an international best seller. (The book was turned into a film in 2009.) A year later, Gaiman teamed with Dave McKean, his partner on a number of graphic novels, to create *The Wolves in the Walls*, an illustrated horror story for children.

The Graveyard Book, another best seller, was Gaiman's first full-length novel for middle-school children. It spins the hauntingly sentimental tale of a young boy who lives in a graveyard and is raised by its many ghostly inhabitants. The book won the Newbery Medal in 2009.

THEODOR GEISEL

(b. 1904–d. 1991)

In 1984 a special Pulitzer Prize was awarded to Theodor Seuss Geisel—better known as Dr. Seuss—for his "special contribution over

nearly half a century to the education and enjoyment of America's children and their parents." This special prize honored one of the most beloved writers of children's books of the 20th century, even though ironically he had no children of his own.

Geisel was born on March 2, 1904, in Springfield, Mass. He graduated from Dartmouth College in 1925. After studying at Oxford University in England and the Sorbonne in France, he left school to become a freelance humorist and cartoonist for several magazines. He worked as an advertising illustrator for the Standard Oil Company of New Jersey from 1928 to 1941 and as an editorial cartoonist for *PM* newspaper in New York City from 1940 to 1942.

During World War II Geisel served in a division of the army that made educational and informational films. Two of the documentary films that he made during this period, *Hitler Lives* and *Design for Death*, later received Academy Awards—in 1946 and 1947, respectively. In 1957 Geisel became founding president and editor in chief of Beginner Books, a company that published books for young children.

Geisel adopted his pseudonym for his first children's book, *And to Think That*

Theodor Geisel, alias "Dr. Seuss," with models of characters he had created. John Bryson/Time & Life Pictures/Getty Images

I Saw It on Mulberry Street, published in 1937. In the next half century he published nearly 50 books for children. His books combine humorous drawings of fantastic creatures with stories told with simple words, nonsense words, and wild rhymes to create a world of imagination that both entertains and educates children. Some of the most popular of these are *Thidwick, the Big-Hearted Moose* (1948), *Bartholomew and the Oobleck* (1949), *Horton Hears a Who* (1954), *The Cat in the Hat* (1957), *How the Grinch Stole Christmas* (1957), *Green Eggs and Ham* (1960), *The Lorax* (1971), *The Butter Battle Book* (1984), and *Oh, the Places You'll Go!* (1990). *You're Only Old Once!* (1986) was written for adults. Geisel died on September 24, 1991, in La Jolla, California.

JEAN CRAIGHEAD GEORGE

(b. 1919–d. 2012)

U.S. author Jean Craighead George combined interesting characters and

stories with solid scientific information, helping young readers to appreciate and understand nature. Her books drew extensively not only from published material but also from her own firsthand observations of animals and ecological systems.

Jean Craighead was born on July 2, 1919, in Washington, D.C. Her father was an entomologist who encouraged his children to learn about nature, and the family frequently raised orphaned wild animals. After graduating from Pennsylvania State University in 1941, Jean reported for various newspapers and news services. In 1944 she married scientist John L. George. Before divorcing in 1963, the two collaborated on several juvenile books, including *Dipper of Copper Creek* (1956), which won the American Library Association's Aurianne Award for best nature writing.

George began building a name for herself as a solo author with the 1960 Newbery Honor Book *My Side of the Mountain*, the story of an urban teenager who learns about himself and nature when he runs away from home and lives in the Catskill Mountains for a year. The popular book was made into a feature film in 1969. George published a

long-awaited sequel, *On the Far Side of the Mountain*, in 1990.

She won the Newbery Medal in 1973 for *Julie of the Wolves*. The book, which was heavily influenced by a trip George took to Alaska, tells of a lost Inuit teenager who must gain acceptance from a wolf pack in order to survive on the frozen tundra. In 1976 the Children's Literature Association ranked the novel among the 10 best U.S. children's books of the past 200 years. George continued the story in the sequels *Julie* (1994) and *Julie's Wolf Pack* (1997).

George also wrote some nonfiction series for children. For example, *The Moon of the Bears* (1967) and *The Moon of the Monarch Butterflies* (1968) are two of the volumes in the Thirteen Moons collection, each book of which concentrates on a different animal. Each book of the One Day series, which debuted in 1983 with *One Day in the Desert*, examines the ecology of a specific location over the course of a single day.

George continued to write both fiction and nonfiction into the 21st century. She died on May 15, 2012, in Mount Kisco, New York.

GRIMM BROTHERS

Jacob Grimm (b. 1785–d. 1863)
Wilhelm Grimm (b. 1786–d. 1859)

All over the world children have grown up with the Grimm brothers' *Nursery and Household Tales*. Almost everyone knows of the fairy tale characters Snow White and the Seven Dwarfs, Rumpelstiltskin, and Rapunzel. The 200 stories commonly called *Grimm's Fairy Tales* have been translated into 70 languages.

Jacob Ludwig Carl Grimm was born on Jan. 4, 1785, at Hanau in Hesse-Kassel. Wilhelm Carl was born on Feb. 24, 1786. They were the oldest of six children. They grew up in Germany when that country was a loosely organized federation of states.

When they were older, the brothers studied law at the University of Marburg. There Jacob studied under the famous law professor and scholar Friedrich Karl von Savigny, who interested him in the legends of the Middle Ages and in the songs of the minnesingers, the German poet-singers of the 12th to the 14th century. At Marburg the brothers were also influenced by Clemens Brentano, a poet, novelist, and dramatist who helped found the Heidelberg Romantic school. He encouraged their love of folk poetry. In 1814 Wilhelm obtained a job in the library in Kassel, and Jacob joined him there in 1816.

Portrait of Wilhelm (left) *and Jacob Grimm, by Elisabeth Jerichau-Baumann.* Staatliche Museen zu Berlin—Preussischer Kulturbesitz

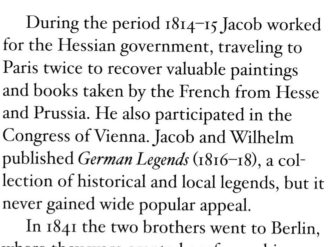

During the period 1814–15 Jacob worked for the Hessian government, traveling to Paris twice to recover valuable paintings and books taken by the French from Hesse and Prussia. He also participated in the Congress of Vienna. Jacob and Wilhelm published *German Legends* (1816–18), a collection of historical and local legends, but it never gained wide popular appeal.

In 1841 the two brothers went to Berlin, where they were granted professorships and elected members of the Academy of Science. Both wrote learned books. Jacob wrote many more than Wilhelm, and his German grammar is one of the world's greatest works in language study. Both worked on a dictionary of the German language—still a classic on historical development and usage—and on the collection of folktales. They spent some 13 years in collecting "from the lips of people" the stories that went into their folktales. The first volume of *Nursery and Household Tales* was published in Berlin in 1812.

While the folktales were intended for children, as the first word of their title suggests, they were not originally told exclusively for children. The Grimms stated in their preface, "As their simple poetry

delights and their truth can interest anyone, and because they remain an inheritance in the house, they are also called House Stories."

In collecting the stories the brothers sometimes drastically edited the tales to stress their point of view with regard to religion, politics, and morality. Frequently, however, the dialect, or local way of speaking, of a particular region was kept so that the stories would not lose their flavor. Sometimes there were several versions of the stories, and these the Grimms combined into one.

The stories were kept alive by the German peasants of the time—the cowherd, the woodcutter, the woodcarver—who had no hope of rising above their positions in life. For someone whose main diet was coarse black bread, it was interesting to hear of a magic table that "satisfied all needs." The tales are touched throughout with the gold that the peasants seldom, if ever, saw—in the form of golden eggs, golden feathers, a tree with leaves of gold. There were good and bad characters and strong contrasts between good and evil. The Grimms stated that "although there is a moral in the stories, that was not their

object, and if it is there it easily grows out of them like fruit from a perfect blossom without any help from man."

After Wilhelm Grimm died on Dec. 16, 1859, Jacob paid tribute to him in the Berlin Academy, noting that the whole of their lives had been passed together. On Sept. 20, 1863, Jacob died.

VIRGINIA HAMILTON

(b. 1936–d. 2002)

During her career as a children's writer, Virginia Hamilton produced original folktales and retellings, contemporary novels, mysteries, fantasy books, and nonfiction. Common to all these works was the author's interest in and respect for African American experiences, history, and culture.

Tales told by Hamilton's parents and other family members during her youth helped her develop an appreciation of storytelling as a way to preserve cultural heritage. She attended Antioch College and Ohio State University in the 1950s and studied at

New School for Social Research upon moving to New York. In 1960 she married poet Arnold Adoff. Her first book, *Zeely*, was published in 1967.

M.C. Higgins, the Great (1974) won the 1975 Newbery Medal and the National Book Award, making it the first work to receive both honors. The novel tells of a boy who searches for a way to protect his family from a strip miner's spoil heap without having to move from their cherished mountain home. Hamilton's Newbery Honor Books include *The Planet of Junior Brown* (1971), *Sweet Whispers, Brother Rush* (1982), and *In the Beginning: Creation Stories from Around the World* (1988).

Among Hamilton's other fictional works are young adult novels, folktale collections, and the fantasy trilogy of *Justice and Her Brothers* (1978), *Dustland* (1980), and *The Gathering* (1981). Hamilton also wrote biographies of W.E.B. Du Bois and Paul Robeson. In *Anthony Burns: The Defeat and Triumph of a Fugitive Slave* (1988), Hamilton blends factual accounts of the main character's trial with fictional accounts of his youth. Continuing her desire to bring African American history into mainstream children's literature, she researched and

retold slave narratives for *Many Thousand Gone: African Americans from Slavery to Freedom* (1992).

Many of Hamilton's works received prestigious awards, including the Edgar Allan Poe Award for best juvenile mystery, the Coretta Scott King Award, and the Boston Globe–Horn Book Award. In 1995, Hamilton received a MacArthur Foundation "genius" grant. She was the first children's author to be so honored. Kent State University in Ohio established an annual conference on multicultural experiences in children's literature in Hamilton's honor in 1984. After a long battle with breast cancer, Hamilton died on Feb. 19, 2002, in Dayton, Ohio.

DANIEL HANDLER

(b. 1970–)

U.S. children's author Daniel Handler is best known for his *A Series of Unfortunate Events*, which he wrote under the pen name Lemony Snicket. This collection of unhappy morality tales was

designed for older children and featured titles such as *The Reptile Room* (1999), *The Austere Academy* (2000), and *The Miserable Mill* (2000).

Handler was born on February 28, 1970, in San Francisco, California. In 1992 he graduated with a bachelor's degree from Wesleyan University in Middletown, Connecticut. After returning to his hometown, he worked as an administrative assistant and a writer for a radio program while writing novels on the side. He then moved to New York City, where he began reviewing movies and reading manuscripts for a literary agent. His novel *The Basic Eight*, which was initially rejected numerous times, was eventually published in 1999. Garnering mixed reviews, the novel told the story of a high-school student who is bludgeoned with a croquet mallet wielded by a classmate. *Watch Your Mouth* (2000), written in the form of an opera, appeared next. As was its predecessor, *Watch Your Mouth* was a dark satire written for adults.

Handler turned to writing books for young adults with his *A Series of Unfortunate Events*. This 13-book series related the travails of three orphaned

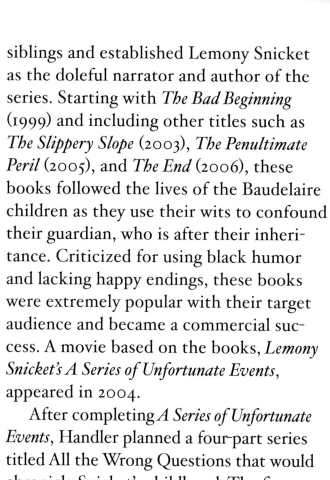

siblings and established Lemony Snicket as the doleful narrator and author of the series. Starting with *The Bad Beginning* (1999) and including other titles such as *The Slippery Slope* (2003), *The Penultimate Peril* (2005), and *The End* (2006), these books followed the lives of the Baudelaire children as they use their wits to confound their guardian, who is after their inheritance. Criticized for using black humor and lacking happy endings, these books were extremely popular with their target audience and became a commercial success. A movie based on the books, *Lemony Snicket's A Series of Unfortunate Events*, appeared in 2004.

After completing *A Series of Unfortunate Events*, Handler planned a four-part series titled All the Wrong Questions that would chronicle Snicket's childhood. The first book of this series, *Who Could That Be at This Hour?*, was published in 2012. Handler's other books included the adult-oriented *Adverbs* (2006), a collection of love stories set in a futuristic San Francisco; *Why We Broke Up* (2011), a young-adult novel about first love; and *The Dark* (2013), a children's picture book.

CHRISTIE LUCY HARRIS

(b. 1907–d. 2002)

Canadian writer and playwright Christie Lucy Harris is best known as an author of books for young readers. Many of her books recount American Indian legends or stories of exploration of the Canadian West.

Christie Lucy Irwin was born on Nov. 21, 1907, in Newark, N.J., but moved as a small child with her family to Canada. She attended the University of British Columbia and taught school for several years after graduating. In 1932 she married Thomas Arthur Harris, and in 1936 she began writing radio scripts on a freelance basis for the Canadian Broadcasting Corp.

Harris began publishing children's books in the late 1950s. Her books on American Indian mythology include *Once Upon a Totem* (1963); *Raven's Cry* (1966), winner of the 1967 Canadian Book of the Year for Children award; and *Mouse Woman and the Vanished Princesses* (1976), winner of the same award in 1977. These critically acclaimed

books sympathetically and accurately depict American Indian cultures of the Pacific Northwest.

Other books for young readers by Harris include *West with the White Chiefs* (1965), a fictionalized account of English explorers crossing western Canada in 1863; *Confessions of a Tow Hanger* (1967), which relates the experiences of a middle child in a family; and *You Have to Draw the Line Somewhere* (1964), about the life of a fashion designer (based on the experiences of her own daughter in the profession). Harris also wrote plays for adults. She died Jan. 5, 2002.

MARGUERITE HENRY

(b. 1902–1997)

The animal adventure stories of Marguerite Henry earned praise from both readers and critics for their realism and suspense. Henry's extensive research lent historical authenticity to her plots, which typically explored a world of wild horses and rugged landscapes.

She was born Marguerite Breithaupt on April 13, 1902, in Milwaukee, Wis. She enjoyed creating stories as a youth, and selling one to *Delineator* magazine at age 11 made her consider a career in writing. After attending Milwaukee State Teachers College for two years, she left school to marry Sidney Crocker Henry in 1923. While the young couple was living in Chicago, Ill., she discovered that she had a talent for putting complicated technical information into plain English and was sought by trade magazines. She also wrote a series of articles on famous men for the *Saturday Evening Post*.

Henry's first children's book, *Auno and Tauno: A Story of Finland* (1940), was inspired by the tales of childhood told by her Finnish cook and the woman's husband. Henry began writing about horses with *Justin Morgan Had a Horse* (1945), a 1946 Newbery Honor book about the origin of the Morgan breed. The book also marked the start of a successful partnership with illustrator Wesley Dennis. Walt Disney Productions adapted *Justin Morgan Had a Horse* as a motion picture in 1972.

Misty of Chincoteague (1947), a fact-based story about two children on an

island off the coast of Virginia who raise money to buy a wild horse and her filly, earned Henry another Newbery Honor award in 1948. In 1961, it received the Lewis Carroll Shelf Award and was made into a feature film. Henry penned the sequels *Sea Star: Orphan of Chincoteague* (1949), *Stormy, Misty's Foal* (1963), and *Misty's Twilight* (1992). The real-life Misty lived with the Henrys for several years.

Henry won the prestigious Newbery Medal in 1949 for *King of the Wind* (1948), a story about a mute stable boy who cares for a neglected colt that eventually becomes the famed Godolphin Arabian and sires three winning racehorses. Henry's other animal stories included *A Boy and a Dog* (1944), *Brighty of the Grand Canyon* (1953), *Gaudenzia: Pride of the Palio* (1960), *Mustang: Wild Spirit of the West* (1966), and *San Domingo: The Medicine Hat Stallion* (1972). She also wrote the fictional biographies *Robert Fulton: Boy Craftsman* (1945) and *Benjamin West and His Cat Grimalkin* (1947), animal nonfiction, and a series of 16 geography books. Henry died on Nov. 26, 1997, at her California home.

KAREN HESSE

(b. 1952–)

The American Library Association honored U.S. author Karen Hesse with the 1998 Newbery Medal for *Out of the Dust*. Like many of her children's novels, it features a young girl in a complex situation who overcomes obstacles to help others and become stronger herself.

Hesse was born on Aug. 29, 1952, in Baltimore, Md. She loved to read as a child and spent much of her time in the library. After studying theater at Towson State College for two years, she left school to get married. She finished her undergraduate studies at the University of Maryland and earned a bachelor's degree in English in 1975. Her early jobs included librarian, typesetter, and leave-benefit coordinator.

Hesse's first published book was *Wish on a Unicorn* (1991). Like many of her works to come, it focused on themes of family and responsibility. The novels *Phoenix Rising* (1994) and *The Music of Dolphins* (1996) were followed by *Out of the Dust* (1997), which was inspired by Hesse's fascination with the scenery she viewed during a car trip

to Colorado. The novel, written in free verse, follows the events in the life of a teenager and her family in Oklahoma during the Dust Bowl of the 1930s. Winner of the 1998 Scott O'Dell Award for historical fiction, the book was true to its period and setting because of Hesse's extensive research. Her other works of historical fiction include *Letters from Rifka* (1992), dealing with a Jewish family fleeing Russia in 1919, and *A Time of Angels* (1995), about a family coping with an influenza epidemic following World War I.

Hesse's books for younger children also often deal with substantial issues. The chapter book *Just Juice* (1998) tackles the subject of illiteracy, while the picture book *Poppy's Chair* (1993) shows a child coping with the death of a grandfather. Hesse's other books for younger audiences include *Lester's Dog* (1993), *Lavender* (1993), *Sable* (1994), and *Come On, Rain!* (1999). Her work was honored by such organizations as the New York Public Library, the Society of Children's Book Writers and Illustrators, and the International Reading Association and by such publications as *School Library Journal* and *Publishers Weekly*.

IRENE HUNT

(b. 1907–d. 2001)

A uthor Irene Hunt also worked as a teacher. Although her books appealed primarily to young adults, they contain fully developed characters who confront realistic problems.

Irene Hunt was born in Newton, Ill., on May 18, 1907. She received an A.B. degree from the University of Illinois in 1939 and an M.A. degree in 1946 from the University of Minnesota. She taught French and English in Oak Park, Ill., from 1930 to 1945, at the University of South Dakota from 1946 to 1950, and in Cicero, Ill., from 1950 to 1965. Her works included *Across Five Aprils* (1964; film 1990), which was a runner-up for the Newbery Medal in 1965; *Up a Road Slowly* (1966), which was awarded the 1967 Newbery Medal; *Trail of Apple Blossoms* (1968); and *No Promises in the Wind* (1970), which won the Charles W. Follett Award and the Friends of Literature Award in 1971. Hunt also wrote *The Lottery Rose* (1976), *William* (1978), and *Claws of a Young Century* (1980).

Hunt's Newbery winner, *Up a Road Slowly*, describes the coming-of-age of a young girl. It reflects the difficulty the author experienced after her own father's death, and it was praised for its sensitive portrayal of its heroine. Her Newberry Honor book, *Across Five Aprils*, tells the story of how one family is affected by the American Civil War.

Several of Hunt's novels were translated into French, German, Italian, Norwegian, and Danish. She died on May 18, 2001, in Savoy, Ill.

NORTON JUSTER

(b. 1929–)

U.S. author Norton Juster began writing children's books in the late 1950s and published his first book, *The Phantom Tollbooth*, in 1961. His works have been adapted into film and stage productions. His book *The Hello, Goodbye Window* (2005), illustrated by Chris Raschka, won a Caldecott Medal for its outstanding illustrations in 2006.

Juster was born on June 2, 1929, in Brooklyn, N.Y. After high school he studied architecture at the University of Pennsylvania. He then spent a year in England studying urban planning, or how cities are created and evolve, on a Fulbright scholarship. In 1954 he joined the U.S. Navy, where he began to write seriously for the first time.

Juster first wrote a children's book called *The Passing of Irving*, which he never published because he felt it was not good enough. Asked by the Ford Foundation to write a children's book about how people experience cities, he researched and tried to write the book but kept getting distracted by a fictional story he had thought up about a bored young boy who goes on a fantastic journey. He eventually decided to write this story instead, and it became *The Phantom Tollbooth*. The book became popular and was turned into a movie in 1969 and a musical in the 21st century.

After leaving the navy in 1957, Juster started his own architectural firm, which he gradually expanded to include several other architects. His firm created the Eric Carle Museum of Picture Book Art and several

buildings for the Colonial Williamsburg Foundation in Virginia. Juster also taught architecture and urban planning from 1970 to 1992, first at Pratt Institute in New York and at Hampshire College in Massachusetts.

Shortly after leaving Hampshire College, Juster retired from architecture and teaching and devoted himself full-time to writing. His books include *The Dot and the Line: A Romance in Lower Mathematics* (1963), *Otter Nonsense* (1982), *As: A Surfeit of Similes* (1989), and *Sourpuss and Sweetie Pie* (2008), which is the sequel to *The Hello, Goodbye Window. The Dot and the Lin*e was turned into an animated film in 1965.

CYNTHIA KADOHATA

(b. 1956–)

Award-winning U.S. author Cynthia Kadohata wrote books that often dealt with the processes of coming-of-age and self-discovery. Having experimented with fiction across many genres, Kadohata found her niche in historical children's novels. Her

book, *Kira-Kira* (2004), was awarded the
Newbery Medal in 2005.

Kadohata was born in Chicago, Ill., in
1956, to working-class Japanese American
parents. Like the characters in some of her
novels, Kadohata lived a migratory life.
During her childhood her family moved
throughout the Midwest and South before
finally settling in Los Angeles. Kadohata
dropped out of high school and began working in restaurants and department stores.
She was accepted into Los Angeles City
College when she was 18 and later trans-
ferred and graduated from the University of
Southern California with a degree in journalism. After graduation, as Kadohata was
recovering from injuries she sustained in a
debilitating car accident, she rediscovered
her love of reading and began writing fiction.

In the early 1980s Kadohata submitted
many stories to various periodicals but was
turned down each time. In 1986, however, the
popular magazine *The New Yorker* accepted
one of her stories. A well-known literary
agent who wanted to turn the story into a
novel subsequently contacted her. Thus the
adult novel *The Floating World* (1989) came
into being. The story was based largely on
Kadohata's childhood. The main character,

a 12-year-old Japanese American girl named Olivia, and her family travel throughout the United States after World War II. Caught between her Japanese and American heritages, Olivia must grow up in a difficult time of uncertainty and cultural isolation.

Kadohata's first children's novel was *Kira-Kira*. *Kira-Kira*, which means "glittering" or "shining" in Japanese, is about a Japanese American girl, Katie Takeshima, who learns to find joy in the small moments and to deal with the difficulties in life after her sister is diagnosed with cancer. The book was highly praised by critics and audiences alike and won the Newbery Medal. Kadohata's other novels for adults include *In the Heart of the Valley of Love* (1992) and *Outside Beauty* (2008). *Weedflower* (2006), *Cracker!* (2007), and *A Million Shades of Gray* (2010) were some of her other children's books.

EZRA JACK KEATS

(b. 1916–d. 1983)

U.S. illustrator and author Ezra Jack Keats won the Caldecott Medal in

1963 for his illustrations for *The Snowy Day*, a book about an urban youth enjoying freshly fallen snow. The book features Keats's trademark collages of solid and patterned paper enhanced by paint.

Keats, the son of Polish immigrants, was born on March 11, 1916, in Brooklyn, N.Y. He loved to draw as a child and treasured whatever art supplies his family could afford. Before being called into service during World War II, Keats worked as a muralist for the Works Progress Administration and drew for a comic-book company. When the war ended, he spent a year painting in Europe. Upon his return home he illustrated various magazine articles and book jackets. An art director at a publishing company hired Keats to illustrate Elizabeth Lansing's *Jubilant for Sure* (1954), and he went on to illustrate more than 30 children's books written by other authors.

My Dog Is Lost (1960) marked Keats's debut as an author-illustrator. The story, which he wrote with Pat Cherr, follows the efforts of a Spanish-speaking immigrant boy trying to find his lost dog. His next publication, *The Snowy Day* (1962), is known for its striking, colorful illustrations as well as for being one of the first children's books

to have an African American lead character in a story without an ethnic theme. This youngster, Peter, was featured again in the 1970 Caldecott Honor Book *Goggles!* (1969) and in the 1970 Boston Globe–Horn Book Award–winner *Hi, Cat!* (1970) as well as in *Whistle for Willie* (1964), *Peter's Chair* (1967), and other books.

Keats also wrote several books about an urban boy named Louie (*Louie*, 1975; *The Trip*, 1978; *Louie's Search*, 1980). His other children's books include *John Henry: An American Legend* (1965), *Jennie's Hat* (1966), and *Clementina's Cactus* (1982). He also edited and illustrated *God Is in the Mountain* (1966), a book of quotations for adults. Keats died on May 6, 1983, in New York City.

RUDYARD KIPLING

(b. 1865–d. 1936)

English author Rudyard Kipling was noted for his tales and poems of British soldiers in India and his stories for children. He received the Nobel Prize for Literature in 1907.

Joseph Rudyard Kipling knew India well. He was born in Bombay on Dec. 30, 1865, when India was part of the British Empire. Beyond the cities and highways of British India, where the English lived, lay strange primitive country. Rudyard and his younger sister, Alice, had an Indian nurse who told them wonderful tales about the jungle animals. These stories remained in the boy's memory.

When Kipling was about six, he and his sister were sent to England to be educated. They were left in the unhappy home of a retired naval officer at Southsea, where the boy was often punished by being forbidden to read. In 1877 his mother came home from India and remade his world. He and his sister were taken to Devonshire to spend the summer with her.

Kipling read constantly—French literature, the English Bible, English poets, and storytellers such as Defoe. In this school also he developed a passionate faith in England and the English people. When he was almost 17, he joined his family back in India, where his father was a school principal. Kipling became a reporter on the one daily newspaper in the Punjab, the *Civil and Military Gazette*. To get material for his

Rudyard Kipling. © Photos.com/Jupiterimages

newspaper articles he traveled around India for about seven years and came to know the country as few other Englishmen did.

Kipling began to write the poems and short stories about the British soldier in India that established his reputation as a writer. Such books as *Plain Tales from the Hills*, published in 1888, *Soldiers Three* (1888), and *Barrack-Room Ballads* (1892) emerged. The slim volume of *Departmental Ditties* (1886) he edited, printed, published, and sold himself.

When his reputation as a writer was firmly established, he married an American, Caroline Balestier, and started off with her on a trip around the world. They settled in Vermont, where their first child was born, and where Kipling wrote the tales that were to make up his *Jungle Books* (1894, 1895). Kipling's father visited them and made the famous drawings that were published first, with the stories, in *St. Nicholas*. After four years in America, the Kiplings decided that their real home was in England. They rented a house in a Sussex village, where in 1897 their only son, John, was born. At his father's urging, Kipling wrote the story known as *Kim*, which was published in 1901.

Many of Kipling's stories draw from his personal experience. For example, *Captains*

Courageous (1897) was inspired by a trip the author made to Glouchester to attend an annual memorial service for the men who had been lost or drowned during the year. Early in 1902 the family bought a house in Sussex Downs that was surrounded by land that had been cultivated since before the Norman Conquest. Thus, stories about Roman times, *Puck of Pook's Hill* (1906) and *Rewards and Fairies* (1910), were begun.

World War I brought personal tragedy when his son was killed fighting in France with the Irish Guards. More and more he withdrew from the active scene, spending the greater part of the year in his Sussex farmhouse. When he was nearly 70 years old, he began to write his autobiography, *Something of Myself*, which was published after his death in London on Jan. 18, 1936. Kipling was buried in Westminster Abbey among England's honored sons.

E. L. KONIGSBURG

(b. 1930–d. 2013)

American author E.L. Konigsburg addressed the important and everyday

problems of children in her award-winning novels and short-story collections. Her talent for creating unpredictable plots and smart, independent characters made her works a popular and critical success.

Konigsburg's original name was Elaine Lobl. She was born on February 10, 1930, in New York City and grew up in Pennsylvania. After graduating with honors from Carnegie Institute of Technology (now Carnegie Mellon University) and marrying David Konigsburg in 1952, she continued to study chemistry in graduate school at the University of Pittsburgh and then taught science at a girls' school for several years. She left her job to raise her three children and began a writing career when the youngest started attending school.

Konigsburg's debut novels were well received. *From the Mixed-Up Files of Mrs. Basil E. Frankweiler* (1967) won the 1968 Newbery Medal, and *Jennifer, Hecate, Macbeth, William McKinley, and Me, Elizabeth* (1967) was selected as a 1968 Newbery Honor Book, making Konigsburg the first author ever to receive both accolades in the same year. Her Newbery winner chronicles the adventures of two runaways who become involved in solving a mystery while hiding out at the

Metropolitan Museum of Art in New York City. The novel was turned into a feature film in 1973 and a made-for-television movie in 1995. Her Newbery Honor Book is about the character Elizabeth's loneliness at a new school, where she does not fit in. When she meets Jennifer, another outsider, the two girls become friends. The idea for the story came from the experiences of Konigsburg's daughter, who had to adjust to school in a new place. Konigsburg provided the illustrations for both works, as she did for many of her books.

Almost 30 years after receiving her first Newbery Medal, Konigsburg won again in 1997 for her novel *The View from Saturday* (1996). The story centers on four sixth-graders who form a successful Academic Bowl team and the paraplegic teacher who serves as the team's coach.

The Child Study Association of America honored many of Konigsburg's works, including the novels *About the B'nai Bagels* (1969) and *Journey to an 800 Number* (1982). Konigsburg was a National Book Award finalist in 1974 for *A Proud Taste for Scarlet and Miniver* (1973), a historical fantasy about Eleanor of Aquitaine. Konigsburg continued to write about famous figures in *The Second Mrs. Giaconda* (1975), a story about

96

Leonardo da Vinci told from the point of view of the artist's apprentice, and in the novel *Up from Jericho Tel* (1986), in which the late actress Tallulah Bankhead summons two children to solve a mystery. Among Konigsburg's later novels were *Silent to the Bone* (2000), *The Outcasts of 19 Schuyler Place* (2004), and *The Mysterious Edge of the Heroic World* (2007).

Konigsburg's short-story collections include *Altogether, One at a Time* (1971) and *Throwing Shadows* (1979). Konigsburg created her first picture book, *Samuel Todd's Book of Great Colors*, in 1990; she followed that with *Samuel Todd's Book of Great Inventions* (1991) and *Amy Elizabeth Explores Bloomingdale's* (1992). Konigsburg also penned the adult nonfiction book *Talk Talk: A Children's Book Author Speaks to Grown-Ups* (1995). She died on April 19, 2013, in Falls Church, Virginia.

JOSEPH KRUMGOLD

(b. 1908–d. 1980)

By winning the Newbery Medal for the year's outstanding children's book in 1954 and again in 1960, U.S. author Joseph

Krumgold became the first writer to receive the honor twice. Krumgold also had an active career as a movie producer.

Krumgold was born on April 9, 1908, in Jersey City, N.J. His father operated movie theaters, and Joseph decided early on to seek a career in the motion picture industry. After graduating from New York University in 1928, he headed to Hollywood and found employment with several major film companies as a press agent, screenwriter, and producer. In addition to more than a dozen film scripts, he penned the adult novel *Thanks to Murder* (1935).

During World War II Krumgold worked for the Office of War Information and developed an interest in documentaries. After the war he lived in Israel for a few years and served as president in charge of production at Palestine Films. His documentary *The House in the Desert* won a prize at the Venice Film Festival. He ran his own production company in the United States during the 1950s and spent the following decade writing, producing, and directing for television.

In 1953 Krumgold made a documentary about sheep farmers in New Mexico

for the United States State Department. A publisher suggested he adapt the film into a children's book. The result was *...and Now Miguel* (1953), a story about a boy who wishes to join the men in his family on their annual sheep drive into the mountains and must prove to his father that he is ready. The popular book was translated into numerous languages, and the American Library Association honored Krumgold with the 1954 Newbery Medal.

Krumgold earned his second Newbery for *Onion John* (1959), a story centering on a boy, his father, and an unconventional old man. The book also won the Lewis Carroll Shelf Award. Krumgold followed with another coming-of-age book, *Henry 3* (1967), which explored suburban family life. His final children's book, *The Most Terrible Turk* (1969), received an award from the Child Study Association.

While many critics praised Krumgold's books, especially for his effective use of first-person narration, some criticized his portrayal of women. Krumgold died from a stroke on July 10, 1980, in Hope, N.J.

ROBERT LAWSON

(b. 1892–d. 1957)

U.S. illustrator and author Robert Lawson holds the distinction of being the first person to win both the Caldecott and Newbery medals, two of the top prizes awarded in children's literature.

Lawson was born on Oct. 4, 1892, in New York City but grew up in Montclair, N.J. After attending the New York School of Fine and Applied Arts (now Parsons School of Design), he worked as a magazine illustrator before serving with the American Expeditionary Forces in France during World War I. He married artist Marie Abrams in 1922, and the two worked together for a few years designing greeting cards. Lawson took up etching during the Great Depression and in 1931 received the John Taylor Arms Prize from the Society of American Etchers.

Lawson first ventured into children's literature when he illustrated the texts of other children's authors, contributing to more than 40 books during his career. Munro Leaf's *The Story of Ferdinand* (1936) helped Lawson gain national attention, and

Lawson cemented his status as a top illustrator with the Caldecott Honor Books *Four and Twenty Blackbirds* (1937, edited by Helen Dean Fish) and *Wee Gillis* (1938, text by Leaf). He also provided the artwork for Richard and Florence Atwater's 1939 Newbery Honor Book *Mr. Popper's Penguins* and Elizabeth Janet Gray's 1943 Newbery Medal winner *Adam of the Road*.

Lawson first assumed the dual roles of author and illustrator for *Ben and Me* (1939). The book follows the life of Benjamin Franklin as seen through the eyes of a mouse. Lawson followed with other books in which a pet reveals the true nature of its famous owner, including *I Discover Columbus* (1941), *Mr. Revere and I* (1953), and *Captain Kidd's Cat* (1956).

Lawson won the Caldecott Medal in 1941 for *They Were Strong and Good*, a picture book about his ancestors. Like many of his works, it demonstrated his talent for line drawings and his interest in encouraging patriotism. In 1945 Lawson received the Newbery Medal for *Rabbit Hill*, a story in which wild animals speculate about the new inhabitants of an old farmhouse. Lawson published a sequel, *The Tough Winter*, in 1954. The posthumously published *The*

Great Wheel (1957), a tale about an Irish teenager who comes to the United States and helps build the first Ferris wheel, was selected as a Newbery Honor Book in 1958.

LOIS LENSKI

(b. 1893–d. 1974)

During a career spanning roughly 50 years, U.S. author and illustrator Lois Lenski wrote and illustrated a large number of realistic, informative books for children. In addition, she created artwork to accompany text penned by others.

Lenski was born on Oct. 14, 1893, in Springfield, Ohio. She became interested in art as a child and often entered her work in local competitions. After graduating from Ohio State University in 1915 with a bachelor's degree in education, she studied at New York's Art Students League and London's Westminster School of Art.

As a freelance illustrator, Lenski contributed to the books of Kenneth Grahame, Caroline D. Emerson, Watty Piper, Maud Hart Lovelace, and others. A publisher who was impressed with her drawings but unable

to link them to existing manuscripts encouraged her to try writing her own stories. This led to her writing approximately 100 books during her career, for audiences ranging from preschool through young adult.

Lenski's fiction for older children tends to be either historical or regional. To give her historical books authenticity, she often pored through diaries, documents, and other material to acquire a knowledge of each time and place. *Phebe Fairchild: Her Book*, a tale about a 10-year-old girl living with relatives in rural Connecticut during the 1830s, was named a Newbery Honor Book in 1937. In 1942, the same honor was bestowed on *Indian Captive: The Story of Mary Jemison*. The book focuses on how conflicts between Native Americans and settlers affect one girl.

To gain ideas for her regional series, Lenski traveled to various places in the United States and lived among the people about whom she wished to write. The best-known book of this series is the 1946 Newbery Medal winner *Strawberry Girl*, a story about a family in Florida trying to make a living from fruit growing.

Before her death in September 1974, she published several books for adults,

including *Adventures in Understanding: Talks to Parents, Teachers, and Librarians, 1944–1966* (1968); *Florida, My Florida: Poems* (1971); and *Journey into Childhood: Autobiography of Lois Lenski* (1972).

ASTRID LINDGREN

(b. 1907–d. 2002)

Swedish author Astrid Lindgren wrote some 100 children's books, about half of which were translated into English. Although best known for her humorous adventure stories—such as her popular tales about Pippi Longstocking—she also wrote mysteries, fantasies, folklore, realistic fiction, and picture books.

She was born Astrid Anna Emilia Ericsson on Nov. 14, 1907, in Vimmerby, Sweden, and grew up on a farm. After completing school she worked as a secretary in Stockholm before marrying Sture Lindgren in 1931. Her children often asked her to make up stories, and she began writing them down while bedridden after an accident. Her first book, *Britt-Mari Opens Her Heart*, was published in 1944.

Pippi Longstocking (1945) introduced Lindgren's best-known character. While many readers immediately took to the adventures of the strong, clever girl with red pigtails and abundant wealth who lives without parents in a small Swedish town, some critics expressed disapproval of her unconventional behavior and lifestyle. Pippi's adventures continued in *Pippi Goes on Board* (1946) and *Pippi in the South Seas* (1948). The books were published in the United States in the 1950s.

Lindgren's other works include *Bill Bergson, Master Detective* (1946), *Mio, My Son* (1954), *Karlsson-on-the-Roof* (1955), *Sia Lives on Kilimanjaro* (1958), *The Tomten* (1961), *Emil in the Soup Tureen* (1963), *Emil's Pranks* (1966), *The Brothers Lionheart* (1973), and *Ronia, the Robber's Daughter* (1981). Several of her books were adapted into movies.

Lindgren's books were translated into more than 50 languages. The International Board on Books for Young People presented her with the Hans Christian Andersen Medal in 1958 for *Rasmus and the Vagabond* (1956). In 1978 she received both the German Booksellers' Peace Award and the Welsh Arts Council's International Writer's

Prize. In her homeland, she was honored with the Swedish State Award (1957), the Swedish Academy's Gold Medal (1971), and the Litteris et Artibus Medal from the king of Sweden (1975). The government also issued postage stamps featuring her characters.

Lindgren worked at Raben and Sjögren Publishers as an editor in the children's book division from 1946 through the early 1970s. After her retirement she devoted considerable time to writing about government reform and animal rights. In 1989 the United States Animal Welfare Institute awarded her the Albert Schweitzer Medal. Lindgren died on Jan. 28, 2002, in Stockholm.

HUGH LOFTING

(b. 1886–d. 1947)

Author and illustrator Hugh Lofting created children's books featuring Dr. Dolittle, a character whose ability to communicate with animals led to many entertaining adventures. The American Library Association awarded Lofting the 1923 Newbery Medal for *The Voyages of Dr. Dolittle*.

Lofting was born on Jan. 14, 1886, in Maidenhead, Berkshire, England. He attended Jesuit boarding school from the age of eight and went on to study civil engineering and architecture at the Massachusetts Institute of Technology and London Polytechnic. After a stint as a surveyor and prospector in Canada, Lofting worked as a civil engineer for railroad companies in West Africa and Cuba. His travels later provided settings for some of his books. He married Flora Small in 1912 and settled in New York City to begin a writing career.

Lofting served in France and Flanders during World War I. While on the front he created the character of Dr. Dolittle to entertain his two young children at home. After he was wounded and sent home, Lofting began trying to get his tales about Dr. Dolittle published. *The Story of Dr. Dolittle* appeared in 1920, and audiences immediately took to the eccentric English physician who begins to treat animals after his abundance of pets drives human patients away. The book, like all in the series, featured Lofting's own pen and ink drawings.

Lofting received the Newbery Medal for the outstanding children's book of 1922 for

The Voyages of Dr. Dolittle. He continued to write books about Dr. Dolittle at the rate of about one a year during the 1920s, producing such titles as *Dr. Dolittle's Zoo* (1925) and *Dr. Dolittle's Garden* (1927). It was widely thought that *Dr. Dolittle in the Moon* (1928) might

Depiction of Dr. Doolittle, created by author Hugh Lofting, at the entrance to an exhibit of Lofting's work at Yale University's Peabody Museum of Natural History, in 2000. © AP Images

be the last book to feature the doctor, but because of popular demand Lofting brought him back for *Dr. Dolittle's Return* (1933). The musical motion picture *Doctor Dolittle*, based on the series of books, was released in 1967. Another film version of the same name, which borrowed the theme of a man who can talk to animals and little else of the original storyline, was released in 1998.

Lofting also wrote children's books in which the doctor did not appear, including *The Story of Mrs. Tubbs* (1923), *Noisy Nora* (1929), *The Twilight of Magic* (1930), and *Tommy, Tilly, and Mrs. Tubbs* (1936). His book-length adult poem *Victory for the Slain* was published in 1942.

Lofting died on Sept. 26, 1947, in Santa Monica, Calif. *Dr. Dolittle and the Secret Lake* was published posthumously in 1948.

MAUD HART LOVELACE

(b. 1892–d. 1980)

U.S. author Maud Hart Lovelace is best known for her popular Betsy-Tacy

books for children. The 13-book series, which won praise for its historical accuracy, chronicles the friendship and lives of three best friends from childhood to marriage in the late 1800s and early 1900s. Lovelace based the stories on her own childhood and friends.

Lovelace was born in Mankato, Minn., on April 26, 1892. After graduating from high school, she attended the University of Minnesota but dropped out for health reasons. While recuperating in California she sold her first story, "Number Eight." She continued writing after moving to New York City in 1921, publishing her first novel, *The Black Angels*, a historical work set in Minnesota, in 1926.

Lovelace began writing the Betsy-Tacy books in 1938. Her other children's books include *The Tune Is in the Tree* (1950), *The Trees Kneel at Christmas* (1951), and *The Valentine Box* (1966). She also coauthored a number of adult books, including *One Stayed at Welcome* (1934), *Gentlemen from England* (1937), and *The Golden Wedge* (1942), with her husband, writer Delos Lovelace.

Maud Hart Lovelace died on March 11, 1980 in California. Several organizations, including the Maud Hart Lovelace Society and the Betsy-Tacy Society, promote her works.

LOIS LOWRY

(b. 1937–)

L ois Lowry was a critically acclaimed children's writer. She solidified her reputation by winning two Newbery Medals in the 1990s.

Lowry was born Lois Ann Hammersberg on March 20, 1937, in Honolulu, Hawaii. She attended Brown University until 1956, when she married Donald Lowry. She returned to school years later and received a degree in English from the University of Southern Maine in 1972.

A Summer to Die (1977), her first juvenile novel, won the International Reading Association's Children's Book Award. The story of a teenage girl dealing with her sister's leukemia, it loosely mirrored the author's own experience of having a sister die young. Lowry continued to weave bits of her past into other works of fiction, including *Autumn Street* (1980), the tale of

Author Lois Lowry, posing outside her summer home. Boston Globe/Getty Images

a girl struggling with traumatic events during World War II. Like the young narrator, Lowry, the daughter of a United States Army officer, moved in with her grandparents during the war.

Anastasia Krupnik (1979) marked the debut of one of Lowry's most enduring characters. Several sequels followed, including *Anastasia Again!* (1981) and

*Anastasia's Chosen Caree*r (1987). Anastasia's little brother took center stage in *All About Sam* (1988).

Lowry won her first Newbery award in 1990 for *Number the Stars*, the account of a young girl and her family helping Jewish neighbors escape Nazi-occupied Denmark in 1943. Her second award came in 1994 for *The Giver*, a novel about a futuristic world without social ills and a 12-year-old boy who questions his seemingly perfect society.

Among Lowry's other juvenile books were *Find a Stranger, Say Goodbye* (1978), *Switcharound* (1985), and *Rabble Starkey* (1987). Her works for adults included literature textbooks and magazine articles. She was an accomplished photographer, and her pictures appeared in her own publications and those of others.

PATRICIA MACLACHLAN

(b. 1938–)

Patricia MacLachlan was the author of several critically acclaimed children's

picture books and novels for preadolescents. She was best known for *Sarah, Plain and Tall*, which won the 1986 Newbery Medal.

MacLachlan was born on March 3, 1938, in Cheyenne, Wyo. After receiving a bachelor's degree from the University of Connecticut in 1962, she worked as a junior high school English teacher. Her first published book, *The Sick Day*, was published in 1979. *Through Grandpa's Eyes* and *Moon, Stars, Frogs, and Friends* followed in 1980.

MacLachlan's fiction tends to be realistic, with a notable exception being the fantasy book *Tomorrow's Wizard* (1982). Plots often revolve around children and their relationships with members of their immediate and extended families. *Arthur, for the Very First Time*, which the Society of Children's Book Writers honored with a Golden Kite Award in 1980, focuses on a boy spending the summer with his great-aunt and great-uncle while his mother is pregnant. In *Cassie Binegar* (1982), the main character laments her family's unconventional behavior, while the protagonist of *Unclaimed Treasures* (1984) struggles with the conventionality of her own family. *Mama One, Mama Two* (1982), the story of a young girl placed in foster care, was inspired by the author's extensive involvement with a family service agency.

Sarah, Plain and Tall (1985; television film, 1991) was recognized by the *New York Times, School Library Journal* and others as one of the best children's books of the year. The novel tells the story of a pioneer man with two children who places an ad for a wife. A woman from Maine comes to their prairie home, but the children fear she may leave them to return to the East. A sequel, *Skylark*, was published in 1985, and made into a television film that aired in 1993.

Among MacLachlan's other books are *Seven Kisses in a Row* (1983), *The Facts and Fictions of Minna Pratt* (1988), and *Journey* (1991). The author has conducted creative writing workshops for both children and adults and served as a visiting lecturer at Smith College.

CYRUS MACMILLAN

(b. 1882–d. 1953)

Canadian educator and writer Cyrus Macmillan was best known for his collections of stories about the Canadian

wilderness for young people. The best of these stories were included in his most celebrated work, *Glooskap's Country and Other Indian Tales.*

Cyrus Macmillan was born on Sept. 12, 1882, in Wood Islands, P.E.I. He was educated both in Canada, where he received a bachelor's and a master's degree from McGill University in Montreal, and in the United States, where he received a master's and a doctoral degree from Harvard. In 1909 he joined the faculty at McGill. He taught there for many years, became the chairman of the English Department, and served as the dean of arts from 1940 to 1947.

In 1918 he published his first collection of short stories—supposedly true tales that he had heard from Indians, fishermen, and sailors—under the title *Canadian Wonder Tales.* A second book, *Canadian Fairy Tales,* followed in 1922. These stories are told almost without dialogue, more in the romantic voice of a professor of English than that of a grizzled woodsmen, and as such they are considered quite readable, though not very authentic.

During his tenure at McGill, he was also occasionally involved in government, serving as the national minister of fisheries for a short time in 1930 and as a member of the House of Commons from 1940 to 1945, during which time he was also the parliamentary assistant to the minister of national defense for air.

After his death, on June 29, 1953, in Fortune Bridge, P.E.I., stories from his two earlier books of folktales were republished as *Glooskap's Country and Other Indian Tales* (1956). This new edition of Macmillan's stories won the Canadian Book of the Year for Children Award in 1957.

GERALD MCDERMOTT

(b. 1941–d. 2012)

U.S. author-illustrator Gerald McDermott gathered tales from around the world and retold them in children's books using straightforward text and bold, colorful pictures filled with geometric shapes and traditional symbols. The American Library Association presented him with the Caldecott Medal in 1975 for *Arrow to the Sun: A Pueblo Indian Tale*.

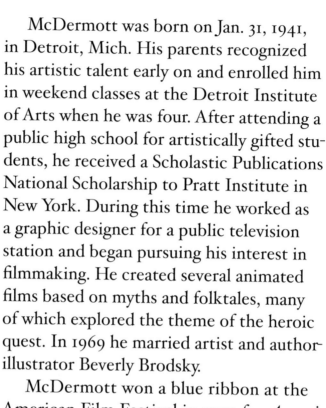

McDermott was born on Jan. 31, 1941, in Detroit, Mich. His parents recognized his artistic talent early on and enrolled him in weekend classes at the Detroit Institute of Arts when he was four. After attending a public high school for artistically gifted students, he received a Scholastic Publications National Scholarship to Pratt Institute in New York. During this time he worked as a graphic designer for a public television station and began pursuing his interest in filmmaking. He created several animated films based on myths and folktales, many of which explored the theme of the heroic quest. In 1969 he married artist and author-illustrator Beverly Brodsky.

McDermott won a blue ribbon at the American Film Festival in 1970 for *Anansi the Spider.* At the request of an editor, he adapted this Ashanti tale into a children's book, and his publication was a runner-up for the Caldecott Medal in 1973. Three other books based on his films followed: *The Magic Tree: A Tale from the Congo* (1973), which received a Boston Globe–Horn Book honor citation; *Arrow to the Sun: A Pueblo Indian Tale* (1974), winner of the 1975

Caldecott Medal; and *The Stonecutter: A Japanese Folk Tale* (1975). His other books include *The Voyage of Osiris: A Myth of Ancient Egypt* (1977), *The Knight of the Lion* (1978), *Sun Flight* (1980), *Daughter of the Earth: A Roman Myth* (1984), and *Daniel O'Rourke: An Irish Tale* (1986). Beginning in 1981 he illustrated numerous texts for author Marianna Mayer.

In 1980, McDermott published *Papagayo the Mischief Maker,* based on a Brazilian folk tale about a mischievious parrot who winds up saving the day in the rain forest. The book was reissued in 1992 and can be considered the first in a series of trickster tales written by McDermott. Other books in the series were *Zomo the Rabbit: A Trickster Tale from West Africa* (1992); *Raven: A Trickster Tale from the Pacific Northwest* (1993), a Caldecott Honor Book; *Coyote: A Trickster Tale from the American Southwest* (1994); *Jabuti the Tortoise: A Trickster Tale from the Amazon* (1995); *Pig Boy: A Trickster Tale from Hawai'i* (2009); and *Monkey: A Trickster Tale from India* (2011).

McDermott died on Dec. 26, 2012 in Los Angeles, Calif. He was 71.

ROBIN MCKINLEY

(b. 1952–)

R obin McKinley introduced new audiences to timeless tales through her adaptations of classic children's literature, and her award-winning original fantasy fiction was treasured by young readers.

Jennifer Carolyn Robin McKinley was born on Nov. 16, 1952, in Warren, Ohio. Because her father was in the military, her family moved often, and she relied on books to be her consistent companions. She briefly attended Dickinson College before transferring to Bowdoin College, where she earned a bachelor's degree in English literature and graduated summa cum laude in 1975. She had been a lifelong horse enthusiast, and one of various jobs she held while trying to establish a writing career was managing a horse farm.

McKinley published *Beauty: A Retelling of the Story of Beauty and the Beast* in 1978. The book became especially popular with teenagers and was honored by the New York Public Library. She went on to retell other classics, including *Tales from the Jungle Book* (1985) and *Black Beauty* (1986).

The Outlaws of Sherwood (1988) put a modern spin on the Robin Hood legend by giving female characters greater and more interesting roles.

The Blue Sword (1982), the first McKinley book set in the imaginary kingdom of Damar, was chosen by the American Library Association as a Newbery Honor Book. She won the Newbery Medal in 1985 for its prequel, *The Hero and the Crown*. Both original adventures center around courageous young heroines whose physical and mental strengths enable them to be victorious in battle, fulfill their destinies, and earn the respect of others.

McKinley also wrote *The Door in the Hedge* (1984), a book of short stories. Her editing credits include *Imaginary Lands* (1987), a collection of stories by leading fantasy writers.

CORNELIA MEIGS

(b. 1884–d. 1973)

The author of more than 30 children's books, Cornelia Meigs is best known for writing historical fiction and

biographies. Her biography of author Louisa May Alcott, *Invincible Louisa*, won the 1934 Newbery Medal.

Cornelia Lynde Meigs was born on Dec. 6, 1884, in Rock Island, Ill., and grew up in Keokuk, Iowa. In 1907 she received a bachelor's degree from Bryn Mawr College; she returned there in 1932 to teach English and stayed for many years. Her first children's book, *The Kingdom of the Winding Road* (1915), was a collection of short stories that evolved from tales she told her young students at the Iowa boarding school where she began her teaching career. She received a Drama League award for her first children's play, *The Steadfast Princess* (1916). *The Island of Appledore* (1917) and some of her other early publications bear the pseudonym Adair Aldon.

Meigs began to display her talent for writing historical fiction with *Master Simon's Garden* (1916), a book about intolerance in a 17th-century Puritan Massachusetts town. An 18th-century adventure, *The Trade Wind* (1927), earned the Beacon Hill Bookshelf prize. She went on to write several more books with historical settings, including *The Willow Whistle* (1931), *Wind in the Chimney* (1934), and *The Covered Bridge* (1936).

The American Library Association began awarding the Newbery Medal for the best children's book of 1922, and Meigs was chosen as a runner-up for *The Windy Hill* (1921). *Clearing Weather* (1928), a story about an 18th-century teenager who revitalizes his family's shipbuilding business, was named a Newbery Honor Book in 1929. In 1933 Meigs was again a runner-up, this time for her tale about a boy during the early days of the U.S. logging industry, *Swift Rivers* (1932).

Meigs finally won the Newbery Medal in 1934 for *Invincible Louisa: The Story of the Author of Little Women* (1933). For this biography, Meigs pored over original material and interviewed the author's family and friends. The book includes photographs and a chronology in addition to stories of how Alcott kept up her family's spirits during hard times. Meigs later edited *Glimpses of Louisa: A Centennial Sampling of the Best Short Stories* (1968) and wrote *Louisa May Alcott and the American Family Story* (1971).

Another biography that Meigs wrote for children, *Jane Addams: Pioneer for Social Justice* (1970), also was well received. Her works for adults include the novel *Railroad West* (1937) and the nonfiction

publications *The Violent Men: A Study of Human Relations in the First American Congress* (1949) and *The Great Design: Men and Events in the United Nations from 1945 to 1963* (1964). Meigs also edited and contributed to *A Critical History of Children's Literature* (1953), which is often regarded as a landmark study of children's literature. Meigs died on Sept. 10, 1973, in Havre de Grace, Md.

A. A. MILNE

(b. 1882–d. 1956)

The author of two books that have immortalized both his name and his son's, A.A. Milne wrote the Winnie-the-Pooh books, perennial favorites about the adventures of toys that belonged to his son Christopher Robin. Although he wrote other books, it is for the Pooh books and two volumes of children's verse that he is best known.

Alan Alexander Milne was born on Jan. 18, 1882, in London, England. He was the youngest of three sons. His father was a shy, quietly humorous schoolmaster. Milne

Winnie the Pooh creator A.A. Milne. Keystone/Hulton
Archive/Getty Images

attended his father's school until he was
11 and then went to Westminster on a
scholarship. He was an able student, especially enjoying mathematics and writing.
Milne edited a university paper while at
Cambridge and graduated in 1903.

Determined to be a writer, he took the
little money he had and settled in London,
where he wrote for newspapers and periodicals. Within two years he was earning
his living by writing, and in 1906 he became
assistant editor of *Punch*. In 1913 he married
the writer Dorothy de Sélincourt.

Soon after his son Christopher Robin
was born in 1919, Milne wrote the books
of verses and stories that are loved by children and parents everywhere. The two
volumes of verse are *When We Were Very
Young*, published in 1924, and *Now We Are
Six* (1927). The humorous storybooks are
Winnie-the-Pooh (1926) and *The House at Pooh
Corner* (1928).

For adults Milne wrote popular plays,
principally comedies, such as *Mr. Pim Passes
By*, first produced in England in 1919, and
The Dover Road, which opened in New York
in 1921. One of the most enjoyable of his
books is his autobiography, *It's Too Late Now*,
published in 1939. The American edition,

called *Autobiography*, appeared the same year. Milne died Jan. 31, 1956, in Hartfield, East Sussex, Eng.

LUCY MAUD MONTGOMERY

(b. 1874–d. 1942)

Mark Twain once deemed Anne Shirley from Canadian author Lucy Maud Montgomery's *Anne of Green Gables* (1908) "the dearest and most lovable child in fiction since the immortal Alice." Generations of readers have shared his sentiment, giving the "Anne" series and its creator a permanent place in children's literature.

Montgomery was born on Nov. 30, 1874, in Clifton (now New London), P.E.I. After her mother's death, Montgomery lived with her grandparents in a farmhouse in Cavendish and turned to books and writing as diversions. As a teenager, she briefly moved in with her father and his new wife, but unhappiness led her back to her childhood home.

Montgomery attended Prince of Wales College and obtained a license to

teach school. Following her grandfather's death in 1898, she left teaching to help her grandmother with her duties as the town's postmistress. Montgomery married Presbyterian minister Ewan Macdonald in 1911, and together they reared two sons.

Montgomery kept journals all her life and accumulated more than 5,000 pages of observations. She drew upon her childhood entries to write her first published book, *Anne of Green Gables*. The popularity of the optimistic, imaginative orphan who shakes up the lives of her new caretakers and other members of their rural village led Montgomery to create a series of books taking the title character through adolescence and adulthood. Other novels include *Anne of Avonlea* (1909), *Anne of the Island* (1915), *Anne's House of Dreams* (1917), *Rainbow Valley* (1919), *Anne of Windy Poplars* (1936), and *Anne of Ingleside* (1939). *Rilla of Ingleside* (1921) focuses on Anne's daughter. Montgomery also published collections of short stories with connections to Anne. The "Anne" series has been translated into numerous languages and has been adapted for stage, screen, and television.

Many of Montgomery's other books also feature unique young heroines, including

The Story Girl (1911) and its sequel, *The Golden Road* (1913); the "Emily" trilogy (*Emily of New Moon*, 1923; *Emily Climbs*, 1925; and *Emily's Quest*, 1927); and *Jane of Lantern Hill* (1937). Her first book of poetry, *The Watchman and Other Poems*, was published in 1916. Many of her other poems, as well as short stories, diaries, and letters, were published posthumously.

Montgomery was named a Fellow of the Royal Society of Arts in 1923 and an Officer of the Order of the British Empire in 1935. She died on April 24, 1942, in Toronto. The province of Prince Edward Island, the setting for most of her books, continues to credit her with enlarging its tourism industry, and various museums and festivals have been named in her honor.

EMILY CHENEY NEVILLE

(b. 1919–d. 1997)

U.S. author Emily Cheney Neville received the prestigious Newbery Medal in 1964 for her first book, *It's Like*

This, Cat. At the time, her use of first-person narration, contemporary dialogue, and an urban setting were considered highly original in children's literature.

She was born Emily Cheney on Dec. 28, 1919, in Manchester, Conn. Members of her large extended family, most of whom worked at the family silk mills, lived close together, and she attended the Cheney Family School along with her siblings and cousins until transferring to public school in seventh grade. At age 16 she went to Bryn Mawr College to study economics and history. After receiving her bachelor's degree in 1940, she worked in the office of the *New York Daily News*. The *New York Daily Mirror* hired her as an office worker the following year, but soon she began writing a daily column. She met her future husband, Glenn Neville, while working at the *Mirror*; they married in 1948.

Neville suspended her career to raise five children and resumed writing when the youngest went to school. After trying to write picture books without success, she expanded a short story she had published in the *Sunday Mirror*. The result was *It's Like This, Cat* (1963), a young-adult novel about a teenager whose decision to get a cat for a pet leads to adventures throughout New York City and to problems with his father.

Neville went on to write other books for children and teenagers, including *The Seventeenth-Street Gang* (1966), *Fogarty* (1969), *Garden of Broken Glass* (1975), and the fictionalized autobiography *Traveler from a Small Kingdom* (1968). The Women's International League for Peace and Freedom presented Neville with the Jane Addams Children's Book Award in 1966 for *Berries Goodman* (1965), a story about a nine-year-old boy whose new friendship is threatened by anti-Semitism.

Neville received a law degree from Albany Law School in 1976 and was admitted to the New York bar the following year. She shifted most of her attention to her private practice but published the picture book *The Bridge* in 1988 and the novel *The China Year* in 1991. She died on Dec. 14, 1997 in Keene Valley, N.Y.

ROBERT C. O'BRIEN

(b. 1918–d. 1973)

As an editor and journalist Robert Leslie Conly used his given name to cover

stories for such publications as *Newsweek* and *National Geographic*. When he wrote fiction, however, he used the pen name Robert Carroll O'Brien. His award-winning fiction for children and young adults is noted for its excellent characterization and its skillful portrayal of the natural world.

Robert Leslie Conly was born on Jan. 11, 1918, in New York, N.Y. In 1935 he entered Williams College in Williamstown, Mass., but he dropped out during his second year there. After briefly studying piano at the Juilliard School of Music in New York City, he resumed his college education at the University of Rochester, where he earned a degree in English in 1940. That year he began working as a journalist for *Newsweek*. Disqualified for health reasons from serving in the armed forces during World War II, Conly moved to Washington, D.C., where he covered national and local news for the *Washington Times-Herald* and *Pathfinder News* before accepting a position with *National Geographic* in 1951. Conly remained active as a writer and editor for the rest of his life.

Conly did not begin writing fiction until he was in his late 40s. His first work of fiction was the children's novel *The Silver Crown*, published under the pen name

Robert C. O'Brien in 1968. He gained prominence with *Mrs. Frisby and the Rats of NIMH* (1971), which concerns a family of field mice that enlists the rats of NIMH—a laboratory-raised breed of superintelligent rodents—to help them out of a life-or-death situation. The novel won the 1972 Newbery Medal and was a runner-up for the National Book Award. In 1972 O'Brien published the suspense novel *A Report from Group 17*, a tale of politics and biological warfare for young adults. The thriller *Z for Zachariah* (1975) tells of two survivors of nuclear war. O'Brien died on March 5, 1973, in Washington, D.C. His daughter Jane Leslie Conly, also a children's author, wrote sequels to *Mrs. Frisby and the Rats of NIMH*.

SCOTT O'DELL

(b. 1898–d. 1989)

U.S. author Scott O'Dell was a prolific writer of books for children. His first Newbery Award–winning book, *Island of the Blue Dolphins*, was followed by three others, as well as many additional novels.

O'Dell was born on May 23, 1898, in Los Angeles, Calif. He attended Occidental

College, the University of Wisconsin, Stanford University, and the University of Rome. He worked as a cameraman and a journalist and wrote five books for adults before concentrating on historical literature for children.

One of his best-known works was his first book for children, *Island of the Blue Dolphins*, which was awarded the 1961 Newbery Medal and which was made into a motion picture in 1964. O'Dell also won Newbery honor awards in 1967, 1968, and 1971 for *The King's Fifth* (1966), *The Black Pearl* (1967), and *Sing Down the Moon* (1970), respectively. His other works included *Hill of the Hawk* (1947), *Man Alone* (1953), and *Zia* (1976).

O'Dell was awarded the Hans Christian Andersen Medal in 1972 and the Regina Medal in 1978. He established the Scott O'Dell Award for Historical Fiction in 1981. O'Dell died on Oct. 15, 1989.

LINDA SUE PARK

(b. 1960–)

U.S. author Linda Sue Park wrote young adult stories that transport readers to

Korea and explore themes of self-discovery, courage, and perseverance. Park was awarded the Newbery Medal for her novel *A Single Shard* (2001).

Park was born on March 25, 1960, in Urbana, Ill., to first generation Korean immigrants. From an early age she was an avid reader and writer. She published her first work of poetry in a children's magazine when she was nine years old. After graduating from Stanford University in 1981 with a degree in English, Park took a public relations position at an oil company while still composing poetry and short stories on the side. In 1983 she moved to Ireland and later lived in England with her husband and children. Park continued to practice her writing—most notably as a food critic, a journalist, and an advertising copywriter—but she ultimately found the work unfulfilling.

Park and her family moved back to the United States in 1990. While pursuing an interest in Korean folktales, Park learned a great deal about her heritage and also discovered that she wanted to try writing young adult books. Her first book, *Seesaw Girl* (1999), is set in 17th-century Korea and tells of a sheltered young girl's curiosity

to see the world beyond the walls of her home. Cultural expectations versus individual desire likewise play a significant role in Park's second book, *The Kite Fighters* (2000). Her third novel, *A Single Shard*, was published in 2001. This piece of historical fiction, set in 12th-century Korea, tells the story of an orphan who defies great odds

Children's book author Linda Sue Park, speaking at the 2012 National Book Festival in Washington, D.C.
Jeff Malet Photography/Newscom

to achieve his dream of becoming a potter. Like Park's other works, accuracy and attention to detail give the book an authentic feel, and timeless topics help young readers to identify with characters that on the surface might seem much different than themselves. In 2002 *A Single Shard* won the Newbery Medal.

Park also published *When My Name Was Keoko* (2002), a World War II-era story of a Korean family living under Japanese occupation. The story mirrors her mother's childhood. Her other works include *The Fire-Keeper's Son* (2003), *Archer's Quest* (2006), and *Keeping Score* (2008). Park also has written poetry and short stories for adults and children's picture books.

KATHERINE PATERSON

(b. 1932–)

H er ability to create fully developed, realistic characters who experience personal growth as they confront difficult

situations made U.S. author Katherine Paterson the winner of two Newbery Medals and earned her many young fans who could identify with her books.

She was born Katherine Womeldorf, the daughter of Presbyterian missionaries, on Oct. 31, 1932, in Qingjiang, China. Her family moved often throughout her youth, and books provided a source of continuity and comfort. After receiving a bachelor's degree from King College in Tennessee in 1954 and a master's degree from the Presbyterian School of Christian Education in 1957, she served as a missionary in Japan. In 1962, she married John Paterson, a minister she met while studying on fellowship at Union Theological Seminary in New York; they had two sons and adopted two daughters.

Feudal Japan served as the setting for Katherine Paterson's first two novels, *The Sign of the Chrysanthemum* (1973) and *Of Nightingales That Weep* (1974). *The Master Puppeteer* (1975), set in 18th-century Japan, won a National Book Award. She further exposed young readers to Japanese culture with her translations of the folktales *The Crane Wife* (1981), *The Tongue-Cut Sparrow* (1987), and *The Tale of the Mandarin Ducks* (1990). Among Paterson's historical fiction set in the United States is *Lyddie* (1991), a story about a millworker in 19th-century Massachusetts. *Jip: His Story* (1996), which takes place on a Vermont farm in the mid-1800s, won the Scott O'Dell Award in 1997.

Paterson received her first Newbery Medal in 1978 for *Bridge to Terabithia* (1977), a book set in modern-day America that deals with friendship and the strength to overcome tragedy. It was made into a movie in 2007. Her next book, *The Great Gilly Hopkins* (1978), was a humorous story about a tough-as-nails foster child who finally meets a woman who knows how to reach her; it was chosen as a Newbery Honor Book in 1979 and also received a National Book Award. Paterson earned another Newbery Medal for *Jacob Have I Loved* (1980), a serious novel about overcoming sibling rivalry. Other contemporary publications included *Come Sing, Jimmy Jo* (1985), *Flip-Flop Girl* (1994), *The Same Stuff as Stars* (2002), and *Bread and Roses, Too* (2006).

Christmas stories Paterson annually wrote for her husband's church services were published as the collections *Angels and Other Strangers* (1979) and *A Midnight Clear* (1995). She also wrote nonfiction books for

Katherine Paterson, upon being named the National Ambassador for Young People's Literature in 2010.
Leigh Vogel/Getty Images

adults on reading and writing children's literature.

Paterson was honored by the Child Study Association of America, the National Council for Social Studies, the International Reading Association, and several trade magazines. In 1987, she received the Adolescent Literature Assembly Award from the National Council of Teachers of English for her overall body of work. The following year, the Catholic Library Association presented her with the prestigious Regina Medal.

SUSAN PATRON

(b. 1948–)

U.S. author Susan Patron was a former librarian turned award-winning children's book author. She was known for her Lucky books, which feature an independent and spirited girl named Lucky. The first novel in the series, *The Higher Power of Lucky* (2006), won the Newbery Medal in 2007.

Patron was born on March 18, 1948, near Los Angeles, Calif. As the middle of three

sisters, she cultivated a skill for eavesdropping, imagining, and storytelling to keep her younger sister entertained. After hearing a reading of E.B. White's *Charlotte's Web* in the fourth grade, Patron determined to be a writer. She obtained a bachelor's degree in English literature and a master's degree in library and information science before starting as a children's librarian at the Los Angeles Public Library in 1972. Later she became senior librarian and began writing her own stories. Patron retired in 2007, but not before publishing several children's picture books and novels.

Patron's first book, *Burgoo Stew* (1991), was a picture book featuring the witty and resourceful character Billy Que. Her next book, *Five Bad Boys, Billy Que, and the Dustdobbin* (1992), saw the return of Billy Que in a lesson about empathy and charity. Patron's books were also inspired by her childhood. In the chapter book *Maybe Yes, Maybe No, Maybe Maybe* (1993), she retells the stories she told her younger sister in their youth. The book won numerous awards and was named an American Library Association Notable Book of 1994.

In 2006 Patron published *The Higher Power of Lucky*, which follows the

adventures of 10-year-old Lucky and her dog after they run away from home and take shelter in the Mojave Desert. The book has been translated into nine languages. *Lucky Breaks* (2009) and *Lucky for Good* (2011), the other two books in the Lucky trilogy, continue to document Lucky's journey through adolescence in the small town of Hard Pan, Calif.

GARY PAULSEN

(b. 1939–)

Gary Paulsen wrote more than 100 books of fiction and nonfiction for young people and adults. He was noted especially for his fast-paced and powerfully written novels for young adults. The Catholic Library Association recognized his literary contributions with the 1995 Regina Medal.

Paulsen was born on May 17, 1939, in Minneapolis, Minn., and was reared by his grandmother and other members of his extended family while his father served in World War II and his mother worked in Chicago. He lived in the Philippines with

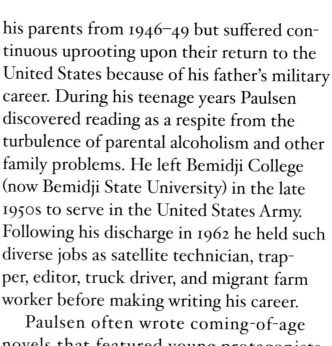

his parents from 1946–49 but suffered continuous uprooting upon their return to the United States because of his father's military career. During his teenage years Paulsen discovered reading as a respite from the turbulence of parental alcoholism and other family problems. He left Bemidji College (now Bemidji State University) in the late 1950s to serve in the United States Army. Following his discharge in 1962 he held such diverse jobs as satellite technician, trapper, editor, truck driver, and migrant farm worker before making writing his career.

Paulsen often wrote coming-of-age novels that featured young protagonists making discoveries about themselves and their world by facing natural challenges. *Dogsong* (1985), the story of an Inuit boy reconnecting with his heritage through a dogsled excursion, was chosen as a 1986 Newbery Honor Book. Paulsen also was a runner-up for the Newbery Medal in 1988 for *Hatchet* (1987), a survival story set in the Canadian wilderness, and in 1990 for *The Winter Room* (1989), a book about farm life in northern Minnesota.

Some of Paulsen's other notable juvenile titles included *Tracker* (1984), *The Voyage of the Frog* (1989), *The Haymeadow* (1992), *Nightjohn* (1993), and *Sarny: A Life Remembered* (1997). He also wrote the popular Culpepper Adventures and the Gary Paulsen World of Adventure series, both of which began in the 1990s. Some of his books featured illustrations by his wife, artist Ruth Wright Paulsen.

Paulsen's passion for sports, nature, and adventure provided a basis for his juvenile and adult nonfiction, which ranged from informational, factual publications to works that recounted personal experiences. His nonfiction titles included *Dribbling, Shooting, and Scoring Sometimes* (1976), *Downhill, Hotdogging and Cross-Country—If the Snow Isn't Sticky* (1979), *Father Water, Mother Woods: Essays on Fishing and Hunting in the North Woods* (1994), *Winterdance—The Fine Madness of Running the Iditarod* (1994), and *Pilgrimage on a Steel Ride: A Memoir About Men and Motorcycles* (1997). The autobiographical *Eastern Sun, Winter Moon* (1993) recounted World War II events he witnessed during childhood.

RICHARD PECK

(b. 1934–)

Young adult readers often recognize themselves in the pages of books written by U.S. author Richard Peck. His willingness to tackle challenging subjects in an interesting yet realistic way brought him both popular and critical success.

Richard Wayne Peck was born on April 5, 1934, in Decatur, Ill. He studied at England's University of Exeter in the mid-1950s and received his bachelor's degree from DePauw University, in Greencastle, Ind., in 1956. After several years in Germany with the U.S. Army, he earned a master's degree from Southern Illinois University at Carbondale in 1959 and did additional graduate work at Washington University in St. Louis, Mo., from 1960 to 1961.

Peck spent many years as a high school English teacher. Although he enjoyed his students, he became dissatisfied with the profession and left his job in 1971 to become a writer. In 1972 he published his first novel, *Don't Look and It Won't Hurt*—a story about unwanted pregnancy told from the point of view of the pregnant adolescent's younger sister. As he did in other books, Peck turned to his knowledge of teenagers—gained in the classroom—to create true-to-life dialogue and scenarios.

Peck dealt with the subject of rape in *Are You In the House Alone?* (1976), winner of the Edgar Allan Poe Award for the year's best juvenile mystery novel. *A Long Way from Chicago* (1998) was a runner-up for the Newbery Medal in 1999. Its sequel, *A Year Down Yonder* (2000), won the prestigious award in 2001. Both books humorously tell of a teenage girl who goes to spend time with her colorful grandmother in rural Illinois during the Great Depression.

Some of Peck's other books include *Dreamland Lake* (1973), *The Ghost Belonged to Me* (1975), *Father Figure* (1978), *Close Enough to Touch* (1981), *Remembering the Good Times* (1985), *Blossom Culp and the Sleep of Death* (1986), *The Last Safe Place on Earth* (1995), *The River Between Us* (2003), *Here Lies the Librarian* (2006), and *Secrets at Sea* (2011). *School Library Journal* and the Young Adult Library Services Association of the American Library Association awarded Peck the Margaret A. Edwards (MAE) Award in 1990 in recognition of lifetime

achievement in the field of young adult literature.

Peck published a few novels for adults, including *Amanda/Miranda* (1980) and *This Family of Women* (1983), and edited several volumes of essays and poetry. His autobiography, *Anonymously Yours*, was published in 1991. He also was the author of *Love and Death at the Mall: Teaching and Writing for the Literate Young* (1994) and of a column on the architecture of historic neighborhoods for the *New York Times*.

LYNNE RAE PERKINS

(b. 1956–)

U.S. children's book author and illustrator Lynne Rae Perkins was known for her ability to clearly and sensitively convey the challenges of growing up. She won the Newbery Medal in 2006 for her second novel, *Criss Cross* (2005).

Perkins was born in Pittsburgh, Pa., on July 31, 1956. She originally wanted to be a children's book illustrator. She received a bachelor's degree in fine arts from Pennsylvania State University in 1978 and a master's degree from the University of Wisconsin at Milwaukee in 1981. Her early jobs included working as a graphic designer. Perkins began writing after an art director suggested that she write her own stories to accompany her drawings.

Taking the art director's advice, Perkins published several children's books featuring her own illustrations and photographs. Her first picture book, *Home Lovely* (1995), relates the story of a young girl who cares for a garden while her mother is at work. This book won a Boston Globe–Horn Book Honor Book Award for achievement in children's and young adults' literature. Perkins' next book, *Clouds for Dinner* (1997), tells about a girl named Janet and her astronomy-loving parents. In it Perkins explores the desires for normalcy and acceptance. In 2002 she published *The Broken Cat* and the following year *Snow Music*, which was also a Boston Globe–Horn Book Honor Book. Her later picture books included *Pictures from Our Vacation* (2007) and *The Cardboard Piano* (2008).

Aside from picture books, Perkins also wrote novels. Her first novel, *All Alone in the Universe* (1999), was honored as an American Library Association

(ALA) Notable Children's Book. It also won a *Bulletin* Blue Ribbon for excellence in children's writing, made the ALA Booklist "Top 10 First Novels," and was a *Smithsonian Magazine* Notable Book for Children. Her second novel, *Criss Cross*, was a sequel to *All Alone in the Universe* and the 2006 Newbery winner. It weaves poetry, prose, drawings, and photographs into a story about friendship and life-defining decisions. *As Easy as Falling Off the Face of the Earth*, about the adventures of a 15-year-old boy, was published in 2010. Perkins also illustrated Sharon Phillips Denslow's book *Georgie Lee* (2002).

BEATRIX POTTER

(b. 1866–d. 1943)

The English author and illustrator Beatrix Potter created Peter Rabbit, Jeremy Fisher, Jemima Puddle-Duck, Mrs. Tiggy-Winkle, and other popular animal characters. Her *Tale of Peter Rabbit*, first published privately in 1900, went on to become the best-selling children's book of all time.

Helen Beatrix Potter was born on July 28, 1866, in South Kensington, Middlesex, England. She spent a lonely and repressed childhood enlivened only by long family holidays in Scotland or the English Lake District, which inspired her love of animals and her imaginative watercolor drawings.

When she was 27, she sent an illustrated animal story to a sick child of a former governess, about four bunnies named Flopsy, Mopsy, Cotton-tail, and Peter. The illustrated letter was so well-received that she decided to publish it privately as The *Tale of Peter Rabbit* (1900). In 1902 it was published commercially with great success by Frederick Warne & Company, which in the next 20 years brought out 22 additional books, beginning with *The Tailor of Gloucester* (1903), *The Tale of Squirrel Nutkin* (1903), and *The Tale of Benjamin Bunny* (1904). The tiny books, which Potter designed so that even the smallest children could hold them, combined a deceptively simple prose, concealing dry north-country humor, with illustrations in the best English watercolor tradition.

Despite strong parental opposition, Potter became engaged in 1905 to Norman Warne, the son of her publisher. After his

Beatrix Potter, 1913. Pictorial Parade/London Daily Express, reproduced by permission of Frederick Warne & Co.

sudden death a few months later she spent much of her time alone at Hill Top, a small farm in the village of Sawrey in the Lake District. In 1913 she married her solicitor, William Heelis, and she spent the last 30 years of her life extending her farm property and breeding Herdwick sheep. She died on Dec. 22, 1943, in Sawrey. She had bequeathed her land to the National Trust, which maintains the Hill Top farmhouse as it was when she lived in it.

ARTHUR RANSOME

(b. 1884–d. 1967)

The British journalist and author Arthur Ransome wrote children's adventure novels noted for their detailed and colorful accounts of the perception and imagination of children. The books also are notable for the picture they present of outdoor life in England.

Arthur Michell Ransome was born on Jan. 18, 1884, in Leeds, Yorkshire, England, and was educated at Rugby School. He worked in a publishing house before becoming a war correspondent in World War I. In

the course of his work he made several trips to Russia, and he also traveled in China, Egypt, and the Sudan. His experiences provided the inspiration for *Old Peter's Russian Tales* (1916) and *Racundra's First Cruise* (1923), about sailing on the Baltic Sea.

Ransome's many other works include *Swallows and Amazons* (1931); *Pigeon Post* (1936), which was awarded the Carnegie Medal in 1937; *We Didn't Mean to Go to Sea* (1937); *Missee Lee* (1941); and *Mainly About Fishing* (1959). Ransome died on June 3, 1967, in Manchester. *The Autobiography of Arthur Ransome* was published in 1976.

ELLEN RASKIN

(b. 1928–d. 1984)

The sense of fun generated by the pictures and words of Ellen Raskin made her popular among young readers. She received several honors during her career,

Ellen Ermingard Raskin was born on March 13, 1928, in Milwaukee, Wis. She grew up during the Great Depression and often read library books and also made up

plays to entertain her family. After studying fine arts at the University of Wisconsin, she moved to New York in 1949. She used the skills acquired during a brief stint at an advertising agency to put together a portfolio and soon found success as a freelance commercial artist. During her career, she designed some 1,000 book jackets and contributed illustrations to accompany the work of writers Dylan Thomas, Edgar Allan Poe, Bill and Vera Cleaver, Aileen Fisher, and others.

Raskin penned her first children's book, *Nothing Ever Happens on My Block*, in 1966. The story and her cartoon-style drawings tell of a young boy who is so convinced that his neighborhood is dull that he is oblivious to the exciting things happening around him. After creating several other picture books, she wrote her first full-length children's novel, *The Mysterious Disappearance of Leon (I Mean Noel)* (1972). Like many of her books that followed, it combined humor, puzzles, intriguing illustrations, and odd characters.

Most notable among the honors Raskin received were the 1978 Boston Globe–Horn Book Award for Fiction and

the 1979 Newbery Medal for *The Westing Game* (1978), a mystery about a murdered millionaire whose heirs are challenged to discover the criminal in order to inherit the estate. *Figgs and Phantoms* was named a Newbery Honor Book in 1975, while *Who, Said Sue, Said Whoo?* was selected as a Boston Globe–Horn Book Award runner-up in the illustration category in 1973. The Mystery Writers of America presented the Edgar Allan Poe Special Award to Raskin in 1975 for *The Tattooed Potato and Other Clues.*

Some of the author's other books included *Spectacles* (1968), *Ghost in a Four-Room Apartment* (1969), *Franklin Stein* (1972), *Moose, Goose, and Little Nobody* (1974), and *Twenty-two, Twenty-three* (1976). Raskin died on Aug. 8, 1984, in New York City.

WILSON RAWLS

(b. 1913–d. 1984)

Wilson Rawls came to professional writing late and published only two young-adult novels. Yet those two books appealed to young people, especially

because of the fully developed animal characters in each.

Woodrow Wilson Rawls was born on Sept. 24, 1913, in Scraper, Okla. He had very little formal education, but his mother read stories to him as a child. He was especially influenced by Jack London's *Call of the Wild*.

Starting when he was a teenager, Rawls went to work as a carpenter, finding jobs in Mexico, South America, Alaska, and throughout the United States. While traveling he wrote stories, but he was hampered by his lack of a formal education. Concerned about spelling and grammar, he mostly kept his stories to himself. With the help and encouragement of his wife, Sophie, Rawls did have his story "The Hounds of Youth" published in the *Saturday Evening Post* in 1961. The story, which had run in three parts in the *Post*, was later published as *Where the Red Fern Grows* (1961; film 1974).

Where the Red Fern Grows was a selection of the Literary Guild. His other novel, *Summer of the Monkeys* (1976), received several awards, including the Sequoyah Children's Book Award, the Golden Archer Award, and the William Allen White

Children's Book Award. Rawls died on Dec. 16, 1984, in Marshfield, Wis.

H. A. REY

(b. 1898–d. 1977)

German-born U.S. illustrator and author H.A. Rey is best known for his *Curious George* series. He created the best-selling, widely translated books about a mischievous monkey in collaboration with his wife, Margret.

Hans Augusto Rey was born in Hamburg, Germany, on Sept. 16, 1898. He grew up near a zoo, and the countless hours he spent there as a boy gave him a lifelong love of animals. He served in the German army in World War I and from 1919 to 1923 attended the universities of Munich and Hamburg, studying philosophy and natural sciences. In 1924 he moved to Brazil, where he worked in his relatives' export-import business and later established an advertising agency. In Brazil Rey also met Margret Elizabeth Waldstein, whom he married in 1935. The next year the couple moved to Paris, where Rey, with his wife's aid, began working on a children's book. The couple were carrying a manuscript of *Curious George* when they fled the invading Germans in 1940. Soon after arriving in Portugal, the couple departed for the United States, where they settled in New York City.

Rey first achieved success with his children's books after arriving in the United States. One of his earliest efforts, *Raffy and the 9 Monkeys* (1939; republished as *Cecily G. and the 9 Monkeys*, 1942), introduced Curious George, who later became the central character of seven of Rey's books: *Curious George* (1941), *Curious George Takes a Job* (1947), *Curious George Rides a Bike* (1952), *Curious George Gets a Medal* (1957), *Curious George Flies a Kite* (1958), *Curious George Learns the Alphabet* (1963), and *Curious George Goes to the Hospital* (1966). The books depict the adventures of a monkey named George and his friend, the Man in the Yellow Hat. Margret Rey's significant contributions to the series were sometimes uncredited.

Rey also published a number of other children's books. Two of the earliest were *Elizabite, the Adventures of a Carnivorous Plant* (1942), about a plant whose appetite

causes numerous problems but that finally wins fame after eating a burglar, and *Tit for Tat* (1942), a collection of poems that encourages children to imagine themselves being treated in the same way as they treat animals. His other books include *Feed the Animals* (1944), *Where's My Baby?* (1950), and *See the Circus* (1956).

Rey had a lifelong interest in astronomy and was an active member of the Amateur Astronomers Association in New York. He wrote two books for amateur astronomers—*The Stars: A New Way to See Them* (1952; for adults) and *Find the Constellations* (1954; for children). Rey died on Aug. 26, 1977, in New York City. The *Curious George* series was continued by other writers after his death.

RICK RIORDAN

(b. 1964–)

U.S. author and schoolteacher Rick Riordan wrote books for both adults and young adults. He was perhaps best known for his Percy Jackson and the Olympians series of books, which blend

Greek mythology with modern-day characters and settings. Many of his books made the *New York Times* best-seller list.

Richard Russell Riordan, Jr., was born on June 5, 1964, in San Antonio, Tex. He first attended North Texas State University (now University of North Texas) in Denton before transferring to the University of Texas at Austin, from which he graduated with bachelor's degrees in history and English. He received his teacher's certification from the University of Texas at San Antonio. After teaching middle school in Texas and California for about 15 years, Riordan quit the profession to dedicate himself to writing full-time.

Riordan began his professional writing career penning mystery novels for adults. These seven books, starting with *Big Red Tequila* (1997) and ending 10 years later with *Rebel Island* (2007), follow the adventures of a private investigator. Riordan started writing for young adults after his son asked him to tell bedtime stories involving Greek gods. After he related all the myths he knew, he began to make up stories, and the idea for Percy Jackson was created. Percy, a 12-year-old boy with both attention-deficit/hyperactivity disorder and dyslexia, is the

main character in seven stories. Early on Percy learns that he is a demigod, and the books recount his adventures. The series included *The Lightning Thief* (2005), *The Sea of Monsters* (2006), *The Titan's Curse* (2007), *The Battle of the Labyrinth* (2008), and *The Last Olympian* (2009). In 2010, the movie *Percy Jackson & the Olympians: The Lightning Thief*, based on the first book in the series, was released.

Riordan's other series of books for young adults included the Heroes of Olympus and the Kane Chronicles. Although the Heroes of Olympus series contained some of the individuals from the Percy Jackson books, the books had a whole new set of main characters. Riordan envisioned the series to include five books, including *The Lost Hero* (2010), *The Son of Neptune* (2011) , *The Mark of Athena* (2012) , and *The House of Hades* (2013). He also published a collection of short stories involving characters from the Olympus and Percy Jackson series titled *The Demigod Diaries* (2012)

Additionally, Riordan is the creative force behind the Kane Chronicles, which involves Egyptian mythology. Books in this series include *The Red Pyramid* (2010), *The Throne of Fire* (2011), and *The Serpent's Shadow*

Rick Riordan, greeting fans at the 2010 launch of his book The Lost Hero *in Austin, Texas.* Sarah Kerver/WireImage/ Getty Images

(2012) . He also has created the overall story line for the 39 Clues series, which tells about two kids racing around the world trying to find hidden clues, beginning with *The Maze of Bones* (2008). This adventure series, which Riordan had originally envisioned as a ten-book series, has taken on a life of its own. It contains books written by various authors and has additional cards and Internet gaming activities to go along with the stories.

CYNTHIA RYLANT

(b. 1954–)

C apable of stirring interest and emotion in readers with natural but well-chosen words, Cynthia Rylant was a prominent author of various forms of literature for children and young adults beginning in the 1980s.

Rylant was born on June 6, 1954, in Hopewell, Va., but spent much of her childhood living in a small town in West Virginia with her grandparents. She received a bachelor's degree in English from Morris Harvey College (now the University of Charleston) in 1975, a master's degree from Marshall University in 1976, and a master's degree in library science from Kent State University in 1982.

While working as a children's librarian, she developed the ambition to become an author. Her first publication, a picture book entitled *When I Was Young in the Mountains* (1982), was chosen as a Caldecott Honor Book; Rylant earned the honor again for *The Relatives Came* (1985).

Rylant received numerous other awards for her work, most notably the 1993 Newbery Medal for *Missing May*, a novel about a girl and her uncle dealing with the loss of a loved one. *A Fine White Dust*, a novel for middle school readers, had been chosen as a Newbery Honor Book in 1987. The National Council for Social Studies and *School Library Journal* both selected *Waiting to Waltz . . . a Childhood*, Rylant's autobiographical collection of poetry, as the best book of 1984.

Among Rylant's other publications were the novels *A Blue-Eyed Daisy* (1985) and *A Kindness* (1988); the short-story collections *Every Living Thing* (1985), *Children of Christmas: Stories for the Season* (1987), and *A Couple of Kooks and Other Stories About*

Love (1990); the autobiography *But I'll Be Back Again: An Album* (1989); and the nonfiction book *Appalachia: The Voices of Sleeping Birds* (1991). A series of picture books about a boy and his dog debuted in 1987 with *Henry and Mudge*. Rylant was also the author and illustrator of the five-book Everyday series (all 1993) for beginning readers.

LOUIS SACHAR

(b. 1954–)

With an ear for classroom banter, an eye for what youngsters consider funny, and a mind that remembers what it was like to be a child, U.S. author Louis Sachar created numerous books that were popular with children. Already known for his Wayside School series and his Marvin Redpost chapter books, he solidified his place in children's literature by winning the 1999 Newbery Medal for *Holes*.

Sachar was born on March 20, 1954, in East Meadow, N.Y., but moved to Tustin, Calif., at age nine. While studying economics at the University of California at

Berkeley, he decided to become a teacher's aide at a local elementary school in exchange for college credit. The experience led him to write stories about a fictionalized school called Wayside, with many characters based on children he met; Sachar himself appears as the lunchtime supervisor known as Louis, the Yard Teacher. *Sideways Stories from Wayside School*, Sachar's first book, was published in 1978. Other publications in the series include *Wayside School Is Falling Down* (1989), *Sideways Arithmetic from Wayside School* (1989), and *Wayside School Gets a Little Stranger* (1995).

Sachar earned a law degree from Hastings College of Law in San Francisco, Calif., in 1980. He practiced law alongside his writing career until the late 1980s, when his books sold enough to enable him to be a full-time author. One of his most popular books was *There's a Boy in the Girls' Bathroom* (1987), a story about the transformation of a fifth-grade bully. Like many of Sachar's books, it deals with the theme of trying to find an identity. Sachar's wife provided the basis for the character Carla, the helpful school counselor.

The character of nine-year-old Marvin Redpost debuted in *Marvin Redpost:*

Picture of Louis Sachar's Newbery Award–winning Holes.
Urbano Delvalle/Time & Life Pictures/Getty Images

Kidnapped at Birth? (1992). Marvin's four-year-old sister was based on Sachar's own daughter, who was that age at the time. Other books in this series include *Marvin Redpost: Why Pick on Me?* (1993), *Marvin Redpost: Alone in His Teacher's House* (1994), and *Marvin Redpost: Class President* (1999).

In addition to his Newbery Medal, Sachar won the National Book Award and the Boston Globe–Horn Book Award for *Holes* (1998; film 2003), a young-adult novel that is substantially longer than his other works. Other books by Sachar include *Small Steps* (2006) and *The Cardturner* (2010).

ANTOINE DE SAINT-EXUPÉRY

(b. 1900–d. 1944)

An adventurous pilot and a lyrical poet, Antoine de Saint-Exupéry conveyed in his books the solitude and mystic grandeur of the early days of flight. He described dangerous adventures in the skies but is

best known for writing the whimsical children's fable *The Little Prince*.

Antoine-Marie-Roger de Saint-Exupéry was born on June 29, 1900, in Lyon, France. In the 1920s he helped establish airmail routes overseas. Saint-Exupéry's first book, *Southern Mail*, was about the life and death of an airmail pilot. It was published in French in 1929. Other books include *Night Flight* (1931), about the first airline pilots, and *Wind, Sand, and Stars* (1939), in which he describes his feelings during flights over the desert.

During World War II Saint-Exupéry flew as a military reconnaissance pilot. After the Germans occupied France in 1940, he escaped to the United States. *The Little Prince* (1943), which in a way is really a children's book for grown-ups, was written during Saint-Exupéry's stay in the United States. A gentle and thoughtful book, it tells the story of a boy who lives alone on a tiny planet.

Saint-Exupéry rejoined the air force in North Africa in 1943. During what was to have been his final reconnaissance mission over the Mediterranean Sea, he died when his plane was shot down on July 31, 1944.

The Wisdom of the Sands (1948), a final volume of reflections that provides insight into the author's views on the meaning of life, was published after his death.

Antoine de Saint-Exupéry, posing in his flight gear. Courtesy of the Bibliothèque Nationale, Paris; photograph, J.P. Ziolo

LAURA AMY SCHLITZ

(b. 1956–)

U.S. author Laura Amy Schlitz was best-known for writing *Good Masters! Sweet Ladies!: Voices from a Medieval Village* (2007), which combined drama and the historical novel to create a series of monologues that offer a revealing look into life in the Middle Ages. She was one of the few playwrights to win a Newbery Medal.

Schlitz was born on Jan. 1, 1956, in Baltimore, Md. She graduated from Goucher College in Towson, Md., in 1977 with a bachelor's degree in aesthetics. Before becoming a librarian and professional storyteller, Schlitz worked as an actress, a playwright, and a costumer. She has written at least eight plays that have been performed at various theaters in Maryland.

In 1991 Schlitz began her work as an elementary school librarian at Park School in Baltimore. For one class project students were told to research aspects of life

in the Middle Ages. To make the project more interactive, Schlitz wrote a series of monologues to be performed by the students. These monologues feature characters ranging from the lord's daughter to the doctor's son to the plowboy and were compiled into *Good Masters! Sweet Ladies!* The book captures the gritty realism of 13th-century England and won the Newbery Medal in 2008.

Schlitz began her writing career with *A Gypsy at Almack's* (1993), a romance for adults published under the pseudonym Chloe Cheshire. Her success, however, came in the 21st century when she concentrated on children's books. *The Hero Schliemann: The Dreamer Who Dug for Troy* (2006) is a biography of archaeologist Heinrich Schliemann enhanced with 19th-century historical facts. *A Drowned Maiden's Hair: A Melodrama* (2006) features a rambunctious orphan girl who gets adopted by a strange family. Other books authored by Schlitz include *The Bearskinner: A Tale of the Brothers Grimm* (2007), *The Night Fairy* (2010), and the Newbery Honor Book *Splendors and Glooms* (2012).

JON SCIESZKA

(b. 1954–)

A merican children's author and educator Jon Scieszka is perhaps best known
for his book *The Stinky Cheese Man and Other
Fairly Stupid Tales* (1992). He also founded
an Internet-based literacy movement called
Guys Read, which encouraged boys to read
and men to serve as reading role models.

Scieszka was born on Sept. 8, 1954, in
Flint, Mich. An avid reader in his youth,
his favorite books was the whimsical *Go,
Dog, Go!* by P.D. Eastman. Scieszka attended
high school at Culver Military Academy. He
entered Albion College with the intention
of studying medicine, but after graduating
in 1976, he chose to study creative writing
at Columbia University, earning an M.F.A.
in 1980. While attempting to forge a career
as a novelist, Scieszka found work teaching
at a private elementary school on the Upper
East Side of New York City. His experiences there inspired him to try writing for
children.

Scieszka teamed with illustrator Lane
Smith to create *The True Story of the Three*

Little Pigs! (1989), a parody of the classic children's tale, told from the perspective of the wolf, who believes he has been unjustly accused of wrongdoing. The book received citations from the *New York Times* and the American Library Association. *The Stinky Cheese Man and Other Fairly Stupid Tales* (1992), a wacky twist on some familiar fairy tales that also was illustrated by Smith, was named a Caldecott Honor Book. Scieszka then quit teaching and devoted himself full time to writing.

Numerous successful titles followed, including *Math Curse* (1995), *Baloney (Henry P.)* (2001), the Time Warp Trio series, which was adapted into an animated program for television, and the Trucktown series. Scieszka's later works included the autobiographical *Knucklehead* (2008) and *Robot Zot!* (2009), illustrated by David Shannon.

In 2008 the Library of Congress appointed Scieszka to serve as national ambassador for young people's literature, a two-year appointment that entrusted him with the task of raising national awareness of the importance of children's books. Scieszka was chosen for the post partly

because he embraced such traditionally "nonliterary" forms as comic books, graphic novels, and the Internet.

MAURICE SENDAK

(b. 1912–d. 2012)

"Children...live in both fantasy and reality; they move back and forth with ease, in a way that we no longer remember how to do." Maurice Sendak, an artist best known for his illustrated children's books, had this to say about children, who were both his subject and a large part of his readership. His understanding of the role that fantasy plays in childhood is a central reason for the wide success of his works.

Maurice Bernard Sendak was born on June 10, 1928, in Brooklyn, N.Y. He developed an early disdain for formal education but studied briefly at the Art Students League. His first jobs included drawing backgrounds for comic strips and creating window displays for toy stores. In 1951 he illustrated *The Wonderful Farm* by Marcel Aymé and a year later Ruth Krauss's *A Hole Is to Dig*. Both were well received, and he

Author Maurice Sendak, posing like one of the "wild things" featured in his most famous book. James Keyser/Time & Life Pictures/Getty Images

went on to illustrate more than 80 children's books.

In 1956 Sendak wrote his first book, *Kenny's Window*, which he also illustrated. In 1963 he wrote *Where the Wild Things Are*, which won the Caldecott Medal. Other books include *Hector Protector* (1965), *In the Night Kitchen* (1970), *Seven Little Monsters* (1977), *Outside Over There* (1981), *We Are All in the Dumps with Jack and Guy* (1993), and *Mommy?* (2006).

In 1975 Sendak wrote and directed *Really Rosie* for television, and several years later he adapted it for a musical. The songs were composed by the singer-songwriter Carole King, and the skits and songs were taken from the four stories of the Nutshell Library, published in 1962. Sendak also designed the sets for other productions, including a 1980 performance of Mozart's opera *The Magic Flute* in Houston, Texas, and a 1983 version of Tchaikovsky's ballet *The Nutcracker Suite* in Seattle, Washington.

In 1988 Sendak published *Caldecott & Co.: Notes on Books and Pictures*, a collection of essays and reviews on writers and illustrators. He was awarded the National Medal of Arts in 1996. He died in Danbury, Connecticut, on May 8, 2012.

KATE SEREDY

(b. 1899–d. 1975)

In little more than a decade in the United States, Kate Seredy transformed from an immigrant who did not know English into a critically acclaimed writer and illustrator of children's books. Her works often centered on themes such as hard work, faith, the interdependence of people, and the beauty of nature.

Seredy was born on Nov. 10, 1899, in Budapest, Hungary. Her father, a teacher, helped her develop an appreciation for books. After high school she earned an art teacher's diploma from the Academy of Arts in Budapest and also spent time studying in Italy, France, and Germany. She served as a nurse for two years during World War I, and the pacifist stance she subsequently developed later influenced her writing.

Seredy illustrated two children's books in Hungary before coming to the United States in 1922. She supported herself in her new homeland by illustrating lamp shades and greeting cards. As her knowledge of English increased, she found work illustrating textbooks and children's trade

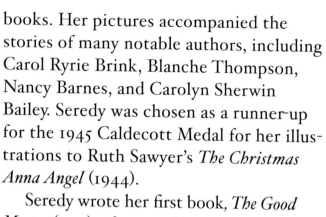

books. Her pictures accompanied the stories of many notable authors, including Carol Ryrie Brink, Blanche Thompson, Nancy Barnes, and Carolyn Sherwin Bailey. Seredy was chosen as a runner-up for the 1945 Caldecott Medal for her illustrations to Ruth Sawyer's *The Christmas Anna Angel* (1944).

Seredy wrote her first book, *The Good Master* (1935), after an editor suggested she try writing about her childhood in Hungary. The story, which was selected by the American Library Association as a 1936 Newbery Honor Book, tells of a spoiled city girl who develops new values while spending time on her uncle's farm. Its sequel, the 1940 Newbery Honor Book *The Singing Tree* (1939), shows the impact of World War I on everyone in the family.

Seredy won the Newbery Medal in 1938 for *The White Stag* (1937), a book based on legends about the founding of Hungary that her father told her as a child. Her other books, all of which she illustrated herself, include *Listening* (1936), *A Tree for Peter* (1941), *The Chestry Oak* (1948), and *The Tenement Tree* (1959). Seredy died on March 7, 1975, in Middletown, NY.

ELIZABETH GEORGE SPEARE

(b. 1908–d. 1994)

Each of U.S. author Elizabeth George Speare's historical fiction books was meticulously researched so that details were appropriate for the period. Her characters were well rounded, and she appealed to her readers by drawing them into history with ease.

She was born Elizabeth George on Nov. 21, 1908, in Melrose, Mass. She began writing stories as a high school student. After studying at Smith College, Speare graduated from Boston University with a bachelor's degree in 1930 and a master's degree in 1932. She later taught English in Massachusetts high schools. She married Alden Speare in 1936; the couple had two children.

Speare continued writing as an adult and was rewarded for her efforts by seeing her first novel, *Calico Captive*, published in 1957. Her sophomore, or second, work, *The Witch of Blackbird Pond* (1958) was awarded the Newbery Medal in 1959. Three years

later, Speare again won the Newbery for *The Bronze Bow* (1961). She also wrote the young-adult nonfiction book *Life in Colonial America* (1963), as well as a novel for adults, *The Prospering* (1967).

Speare's last children's novel, *Sign of the Beaver* (1983), was selected as a Newbery Honor Book and won the Scott O'Dell Award for historical fiction. In 1989 she received the Laura Ingalls Wilder Award for her contributions to children's literature. Speare died on Nov. 15 , 1994, in Tucson, Ariz.

ARMSTRONG SPERRY

(b. 1897–d. 1976)

U.S. author and illustrator Armstrong Sperry is best known for the 1941 Newbery Medal winner *Call It Courage*. The novel is a coming-of-age story about a Polynesian boy who confronts his fear of the sea in order to prove himself to his father and the community.

Armstrong Wells Sperry was born on Nov. 7, 1897, in New Haven, Conn. He

served in the United States Navy in 1917 and studied at the Yale School of Fine Arts, New York's Art Students League, and Colorassi's Academy in Paris between 1918 and 1922. Intrigued since childhood by the stories his great-grandfather told about being a sailor in the South Pacific, Sperry left his job at an advertising agency in 1925 to become an assistant ethnologist on a two-year expedition sponsored by a Hawaiian museum. The experience had a profound effect on his writing, serving as inspiration for *Call It Courage*.

Sperry's *All Sail Set* was chosen as a Newbery Honor Book in 1936. The piece of historical fiction focuses on the *Flying Cloud*, a real 1840s clipper ship. Some of Sperry's other books include *Wagons Westward* (1936), *Little Eagle, A Navajo Boy* (1938), *Lost Lagoon* (1939), *Storm Canvas* (1944), *Danger to Windward* (1947), *The Rain Forest* (1947), *Black Falcon* (1949), *Thunder Country* (1952), and *South of Cape Horn* (1958). Sperry also wrote some nonfiction books, including *Pacific Islands Speaking* (1955) and *All About the Jungle* (1959).

In addition to illustrating his own books, Sperry contributed to the works

of Helen Follett, Clara Ingram Judson, Howard Pease, and other writers. Agnes Hewes's 1937 Newbery Honor Book *The Codfish Musket* also contains illustrations by Sperry. He died on April 26, 1976, in Hanover, N.H.

JERRY SPINELLI

(b. 1941–)

A talent for turning common situations of childhood and adolescence into enjoyable, sometimes humorous, narratives made Jerry Spinelli popular with young readers beginning in the 1980s.

Spinelli was born on Feb. 1, 1941, in Norristown, Pa. He received a bachelor's degree from Gettysburg College in 1963 and a master's degree from Johns Hopkins University in 1964. From the mid-1960s through the 1980s, he worked as an editor for a magazine publishing company; he also served in the United States Naval Reserve from 1966 to 1972.

The father of seven children, Spinelli often got story ideas from events in their lives. He also drew on memories from his own childhood. Spinelli's first book, *Space Station Seventh Grade*, was published in 1982. He later produced a sequel, *Jason and Marceline* (1986), set in the ninth grade. Among his other books were *Who Put That Hair in My Toothbrush?* (1984), *Dump Days* (1988), *There's a Girl in My Hammerlock* (1991), and *Fourth Grade Rats* (1991). The use of profanity and sexual situations in some of his books has been both praised and criticized; some find the realism refreshing and helpful in creating identifiable characters, while others deem it vulgar.

Spinelli received a Newbery Medal in 1991 for *Maniac Magee* (1990), a fable about a runaway orphan with extraordinary athletic abilities. The book was commended for tackling issues such as racism and family problems in ways understandable to middle-grade students.

JOHANNA SPYRI

(b. 1827–d. 1901)

*H**eidi* (published in two parts, 1880-81), the story of a young orphan who lives

in the Swiss mountains with her grandfather, has delighted generations of children. In writing *Heidi* and other stories of life in the mountains of Switzerland, Johanna Spyri drew upon the memories of her own happy childhood.

Johanna Heusser was born on July 12, 1827, in Hirzel, near Zürich, Switzerland. The Heusser home was on the high Swiss Plateau, overlooking Lake Zürich. Beyond it lay Alpine pastures and towering mountain peaks. In this idyllic setting Johanna spent the first 25 years of her life. In 1852 she married Bernhard Spyri, a young lawyer, and moved to Zürich. The Spyris had one son, who died in childhood.

When Spyri was 43 years old, she began to write stories about the people and scenes of her youth. The wholesome tales brought international fame to the Swiss homemaker. Although originally written in German, *Heidi* has been translated into many languages and has been the subject of several motion pictures. In addition to *Heidi*, her books include *The Little Alpine Musician*, *Uncle Titus*, *Gritli*, and *Veronica*.

Spyri lived almost in isolation after her husband's death in 1884. She died in Zürich on July 7, 1901.

REBECCA STEAD

(b. 1968–)

U.S. author Rebecca Stead stumbled into the world of children's literature and has been welcomed there ever since. A former lawyer and public defender, Stead has thus far written only two young adult books, the second of which won the Newbery Medal in 2010.

Stead was born in New York City on Jan. 16, 1968. As a child, she was constantly on the wait for her magical powers to manifest. When they failed to appear, Stead turned to books, where she found a different sort of magic that was more probable. In 1989 she graduated from Vassar College with a bachelor's degree, and in 1994 she obtained a law degree from New York University. Stead worked as a public defender and did some writing on the side.

After her young son accidentally broke her laptop and all her previous adult-oriented writing was lost, Stead decided that it was time to find something new to write about. After rereading the books that she enjoyed as a child, she discovered her passion for writing books for young adults.

Her first book, *First Light* (2007), was inspired by an article that Stead read. The book is centered on the adventures of a 12-year-old boy in Greenland. The novel is the meeting point of fantasy, adventure, and scientific findings about climate change. Stead's second novel, *When You Reach Me* (2009), is about a girl named Miranda living in New York City. Miranda's life takes an unexpected turn when she starts receiving mysterious letters warning her of imminent danger. *When You Reach Me* won the Newbery Medal in 2010.

MILDRED TAYLOR

(b. 1943–)

D rawing upon her own experiences and those of family members, Mildred Taylor created several books of historical fiction for children that offer realistic portraits of black families in the mid-1900s.

Mildred DeLois Taylor was born on Sept. 13, 1943, in Jackson, Miss., but her family moved to Toledo, Ohio, when she was three months old. She grew up hearing her father and other family members tell stories about ancestors. These accounts of people who kept their dignity and spirit in the face of slavery and other injustices contrasted with the limited, often bland, information presented in her textbooks. She vowed to find a way to present a richer portrait of African American life.

After receiving a bachelor's degree in education from the University of Toledo in 1965, Taylor worked with the Peace Corps in Ethiopia and then went to the University of Colorado to earn a master's degree in journalism. While attempting to establish a writing career, she worked as a study-skills coordinator in a black education program that she helped design.

Taylor was first published after winning a contest sponsored by the Council on Interracial Books for Children. *Song of the Trees* (1975) introduced the Logans, a loving, strong, African American family living in Mississippi in the 1930s. She continued their struggle for courage in the face of racial adversity in *Roll of Thunder, Hear My Cry* (1976), which won the Newbery Medal in 1977 and was a finalist for the National Book Award. The novel was adapted into a television miniseries in 1978.

Taylor's next three publications about the Logan family—*Let the Circle Be Unbroken* (1981), *The Friendship* (1987), and *The Road to*

Memphis (1990), all earned the Coretta Scott King Award. Although most of the Logan family stories are told from the perspective of willful daughter Cassie, *Mississippi Bridge* (1990) is told from the point of view of Jeremy Simms, a white character introduced in earlier books.

Several of Taylor's novels were honored by the *New York Times*, including *The Gold Cadillac* (1987), a story about a 1950s family facing racism as they travel from Ohio to Mississippi to visit relatives. The book was inspired by the author's own recollections of traveling back roads to avoid encountering racist police officers and of the family packing their own food for the journey because they were not welcome in Southern restaurants.

HENDRIK VAN LOON

(b. 1882–d. 1944)

U.S. historian and illustrator Hendrik Willem van Loon was the first recipient of the American Library Association's

Newbery Medal, a prestigious honor recognizing excellence in children's literature. He received the award for *The Story of Mankind*, a self-illustrated history of the world through 1920.

Van Loon was born on Jan. 14, 1882, in Rotterdam, The Netherlands, and attended several boarding schools as a youth. His mother died in 1900, and ongoing problems with his father contributed to his decision to come to the United States in 1902. He studied law as an undergraduate at Cornell University in preparation for a career in journalism. After receiving a bachelor's degree in 1905, he worked for the Associated Press. In 1906 he married Eliza Bowditch, and they went on to have two sons. The marriage later dissolved, as did two subsequent marriages.

Van Loon received a doctorate in history from the University of Munich in 1911 and turned his dissertation into the book *The Fall of the Dutch Republic* (1913). For the next several years he lectured at various universities in the United States and worked on books and articles. He served as an associate editor for the *Baltimore Sun* from 1923 to 1924 and became a radio commentator in the 1930s.

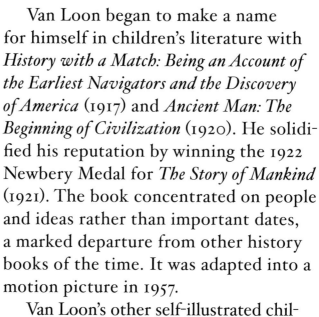

Van Loon began to make a name for himself in children's literature with *History with a Match: Being an Account of the Earliest Navigators and the Discovery of America* (1917) and *Ancient Man: The Beginning of Civilization* (1920). He solidified his reputation by winning the 1922 Newbery Medal for *The Story of Mankind* (1921). The book concentrated on people and ideas rather than important dates, a marked departure from other history books of the time. It was adapted into a motion picture in 1957.

Van Loon's other self-illustrated children's publications include *The Story of the Bible* (1923), *Van Loon's Geography* (1932), *Around the World with the Alphabet* (1935), *Thomas Jefferson: The Serene Citizen from Monticello* (1943), and *The Life and Times of Simon Bolivar* (1943). He also worked on songbooks with musician Grace Castagnetta and illustrated books by other authors. His publications for adults include *R. v. R.: The Life and Times of Rembrandt van Rijn* (1930), *The Arts* (1937), and *Van Loon's Lives* (1942).

Van Loon was made an Officer of the Order of Orange Nassau in 1937, and Queen Wilhelmina conferred upon him

the Order of the Netherlands Lion in 1942. Van Loon died on March 11, 1944, in Old Greenwich, Conn. His unfinished autobiography, *Report to St. Peter*, was published posthumously in 1947. His son Gerard published the book *The Story of Hendrik Willem van Loon* in 1972.

CYNTHIA VOIGT

(b. 1942–)

U.S. author Cynthia Voigt wrote fiction for children and young adults. She was praised for her strong characterizations and for her careful style of writing.

She was born Cynthia Irving on Feb. 25, 1942, in Boston, Mass. She studied at Smith College, receiving a B.A. in 1963, and taught high school English in Maryland from 1965 to 1967, and from 1968 to 1981 at the Key School in Annapolis. In 1974 she married Walter Voigt.

Cynthia Voigt's first novel, *Homecoming* (1981), was nominated for an American Book Award. The book is the story of a young girl named Dicey and her siblings, who are abandoned by their mother. The

sequel to *Homecoming, Dicey's Song* (1982), won a Newbery Medal. Her book *A Solitary Blue* (1983) was named a Newbery Honor Book. All three were part of a series of interconnected stories known as the Tillerman Cycle.

Other stand-alone novels by Voigt include *Tell Me If the Lovers Are Losers* (1982), which told the story of several girls of widely different backgrounds who learn from one another as they form a volleyball team in college, and *The Callendar Papers* (1983).

E. B. WHITE

(b. 1899–d. 1985)

Although E.B. White wrote numerous essays, books, and poems for adults, he is perhaps best known for writing three well-known children's books. Whatever the format or genre, White's works consistently display eloquent craftsmanship and a keen sense of observation.

Elwyn Brooks White was born on July 11, 1899, in Mount Vernon, New York. He attended Cornell University on a scholarship and served as editor in chief of its daily

newspaper. After receiving a bachelor's degree in English in 1921, he worked for the United Press, the American Legion News Service, and the *Seattle Times*. He took a job as a mess boy aboard an Alaskan ship in 1923 but returned to Mount Vernon later in the year to work in an advertising agency.

The founding of *The New Yorker* magazine in 1925 proved pivotal to White's career. After having several submissions accepted, he joined the staff full-time in 1927. He married one of the editors, Katharine Sergeant Angell, in 1929 and became stepfather to her two children; a son was born to them the following year. Although the couple later left New York for a Maine farm, White remained a lifelong contributor to the magazine. He also wrote a monthly column entitled "One Man's Meat" for *Harper's* magazine from 1938 to 1943.

White's publications for adults included *The Lady Is Cold* (1929), *Is Sex Necessary?* (1929, with James Thurber), *Farewell to Model T* (1936), *The Fox of Peapack and Other Poems* (1938), *The Wild Flag* (1946), *The Second Tree from the Corner* (1954), and *The Points of My Compass* (1962). *Letters of E.B. White* was published in 1976, and a collection of his essays appeared a year later. White also

E.B. White. Encyclopædia Britannica, Inc.

contributed to, revised, and eventually had his surname attached to several editions of William Strunk Jr.'s classic writer's manual, *The Elements of Style*.

White's first children's book was *Stuart Little* (1945; film 1999), an adventure story about a 2-inch-tall (5 centimetre), mouselike son born to average human parents. He followed the success of that book with *Charlotte's Web* (1952), winner of the 1958 Lewis Carroll Shelf Award and runner-up for the 1953 Newbery Medal. The book tells of a small pig whose life is spared twice, first by a farmer's daughter and later by the ingenuity of a friendly spider. White drew inspiration for the tale from observing his own farm animals. The book was adapted into an animated film in 1972; a live-action film version was released in 2008.

White's final children's book, *The Trumpet of the Swan* (1970), chronicles the life of a mute trumpeter swan who learns to communicate by writing on a slate and by playing a trumpet. It was nominated for the National Book Award in 1971 and was included on the 1972 International Board on Books for Young People Honor List.

White received a multitude of honors, including the Presidential Medal of Freedom (1963), the Laura Ingalls Wilder Award (1970), and the National Medal for Literature (1971). In 1978 he was awarded a Pulitzer Prize special citation for his body of work. He died in North Brooklin, Maine, on October 1, 1985.

LAURA INGALLS WILDER

(b. 1867–d. 1957)

When she was in her 60s, U.S. author Laura Ingalls Wilder took her daughter's advice and began writing about her life as a pioneer child. The resulting "Little House" books became classics in children's literature not only for their insight into what it was like to grow up on the American frontier during the 1870s and 1880s, but also for their entertainment value.

Laura Elizabeth Ingalls was born on Feb. 7, 1867, in Pepin, Wis. Passage of the Homestead Act led her family to move west during her childhood, and she attended schools in Walnut Grove, Minn.; Burr Oak, Iowa; and De Smet, Dakota Territory. The Ingalls family faced numerous obstacles as they tried to settle, including a malaria outbreak, conflicts with Indians, a grasshopper plague that destroyed their crops, and a seven-month blizzard that prevented the arrival of a train with crucial winter supplies. Before marrying Almanzo Wilder in 1885, Laura taught at a country school and helped pay for her sister Mary to attend a college for the blind.

The Wilders farmed in Dakota Territory. In 1890, after a difficult period when their infant son died and their house was destroyed by fire, the Wilders and their daughter, Rose, moved to Minnesota to live briefly with Almanzo's parents. Following a stay in Florida, where they went so that Almanzo could recover from a diphtheria attack, they returned to De Smet in 1892. In 1894 they made Mansfield, Mo., their permanent home.

In about 1911 Wilder began writing articles for *The Missouri Ruralist* and other publications. She also got involved with many community projects and founded the Mansfield Farm Loan Association. In the late 1920s she began writing about her childhood. *Little House in the Big Woods*, the first book in what became her "Little House" series, was published in 1932. It introduced readers to the Ingalls family and described their life in Wisconsin. She followed that with *Farmer Boy* (1933), a book about Almanzo's childhood, before beginning the story of her family's westward journey in *Little House on the Prairie* (1935). The rest of the books in the series—*On the*

Banks of Plum Creek (1937), *By the Shores of Silver Lake* (1939), *The Long Winter* (1940), *Little Town on the Prairie* (1941), and *These Happy Golden Years* (1943)—were all chosen as Newbery Honor Books.

The First Four Years (1971), a book about Laura and Almanzo's early years of marriage, was published from an unpolished first draft 14 years after Wilder's death on Feb. 10, 1957. Rose Wilder Lane, who helped her mother craft and promote her novels, edited her mother's travel diary for *On the Way Home: The Diary of a Trip from South Dakota to Mansfield, Missouri, in 1894* (1962).

The American Library Association honored Wilder in 1954 by establishing the Laura Ingalls Wilder Medal, which is awarded every three years to an American author or illustrator who has made a lasting contribution to children's literature. Wilder's books have been translated into dozens of languages. Libraries, schools, and roads have been named in her honor, and her former homes are tourist attractions. *Little House on the Prairie*, a popular television series inspired by her books, ran from 1974 to 1983. Wilder died on Feb. 10. 1957, in Mansfield, Mo.

Modern edition of Laura Ingalls Wilder's Little House in the Big Woods, *part of the author's "Little House" series of books.* Jay Colton/Time & Life Pictures/Getty Images

ELIZABETH YATES

(b. 1905–d. 2001)

U.S. author Elizabeth Yates wrote some 50 books during her career, the majority of which were for children. Her works, known for their vivid descriptions, often reveal her Christian faith and her love for people and nature.

Yates was born on Dec. 6, 1905, in Buffalo, N.Y. She was an avid reader during her youth and also enjoyed writing stories and diary entries. At age 20 she moved to New York City, where she held various jobs while trying to establish herself as a professional writer. She married William McGreal in 1929, and the couple lived abroad for the next ten years. During this period she began selling travel articles and celebrity interviews to British and U.S. publications. A mountain-climbing trip in Switzerland inspired her first children's book, *High Holiday*, which was published in England in 1938. Its success led to the sequel *Climbing Higher* (1939), released in the United States in 1940 as *Quest in the North-land*.

Yates continued to write children's books after she and her husband settled in New Hampshire. Her own experiences often provided material for her work. *Patterns on the Wall* (1943) came about when Yates discovered stenciling behind the wallpaper in her new house. A neighbor with a pet lamb served as the inspiration for the 1944 Newbery Honor Book *Mountain Born* (1943); she later wrote a sequel, *A Place for Peter* (1952). A century-old American Indian doll given to her by a friend sparked Yates to create *Carolina's Courage* (1964), a story in which a doll plays a vital role in the safety of a pioneer family.

Yates won the 1951 Newbery Medal for her fact-based book *Amos Fortune, Free Man* (1950). Intrigued after viewing this former slave's gravestone outside of a building where she was to attend a meeting, she began researching his life and how he helped others buy their freedom. Yates also wrote the biographies *Prudence Crandall, Woman of Courage* (1955) and *Pebble in a Pool: The Widening Circles of Dorothy Canfield Fisher's Life* (1958).

The true story *Skeezer, Dog with a Mission* (1973) was made into a television film in 1981. Among her other nonfiction books are *Rainbow 'round the World: A Story of UNICEF* (1954) and the

autobiographies *My Diary—My World* (1981), *My Widening World* (1983), and *One Writer's Way* (1984). *The Lighted Heart* (1960) discusses her husband's blindness. *Someday You'll Write* (1962) provides advice for aspiring young writers.

Yates also wrote several adult novels and edited the works of British folklorist Enys Tregarthen and Scottish writer George MacDonald. She lectured at many writers' conferences and received honorary degrees from several colleges. In 1970 she was given the Sarah Josepha Hale Award as a distinguished New England author. Yates died on July 29, 2001, in Concord, N.H.

JANE YOLEN

(b. 1939–)

A lthough she was perhaps best known for her literary folk and fairy tales, prolific writer Jane Yolen wrote about 200 books in a number of genres. Her works included picture books, children's poetry, nonfiction, science fiction, plays, young adult fiction, and adult novels. The Catholic

Library Association recognized her accomplishments with the 1992 Regina Medal.

Jane Hyatt Yolen was born on February 11, 1939, in New York City but moved to Westport, Connecticut, as a teenager. She won awards for poetry and journalism while attending Smith College and made money by singing folksongs at social events. Following graduation in 1960, she lived in Greenwich Village and worked in publishing until she embarked on a full-time professional writing career in the mid-1960s. She married David Stemple in 1962, and they had the first of their three children in 1966. In 1976 she earned a master's degree in education from the University of Massachusetts.

Pirates in Petticoats (1963), a nonfiction book about female pirates, marked Yolen's entry into children's literature. Her other nonfiction works included *World on a String: The Story of Kites* (1968) and *Friend: The Story of George Fox and the Quakers* (1972). She published her first book of children's verse, *See This Little Line?*, in 1963 as well. Her other collections of verse included *How Beastly!: A Menagerie of Nonsense Poems* (1980), *The Three Bears Rhyme Book* (1987), and *Sea Watch* (1996).

Yolen's Commander Toad science-fiction series and Piggins stories about a mystery-solving pig were popular among young readers. Her extensive body of juvenile fiction also included *No Bath Tonight* (1978), *The Giants Go Camping* (1979), *Mice on Ice* (1980), *The Boy Who Spoke Chimp* (1981), *Letting Swift River Go* (1990), and *Child of Faerie, Child of Earth* (1997). *The Emperor and the Kite* (1967), with illustrations by Ed Young, was selected as a 1968 Caldecott Honor Book. It also won the Lewis Carroll Shelf Award, as did *The Girl Who Loved the Wind* (1972). *The Girl Who Cried Flowers and Other Tales* (1974) was a National Book Award nominee and received the Society of Children's Book Writers' Golden Kite Award. Yolen won the Christopher Medal for *The Seeing Stick* (1977). John Schoenherr captured the 1988 Caldecott Medal for his illustrations to Yolen's *Owl Moon* (1987).

Yolen became interested in young-adult fiction as her own children grew, and she authored titles such as *The Gift of Sarah Barker* (1981), *Dragon's Blood* (1982), and *The Devil's Arithmetic* (1988). Her adult works included *Cards of Grief* (1984) and other pieces of fiction as well as several nonfiction publications about writing children's books.

Yolen helped found the Western New England Storytellers Guild, the Western Massachusetts Illustrators Guild, and the Bay State Writers Guild. She also served in leadership positions for the Society of Children's Book Writers, the Science Fiction Writers of America, and other literary organizations. She lectured at Smith College and conducted workshops for aspiring writers throughout the United States. In 1988 she became the editor of the imprint Jane Yolen Books for Harcourt Brace.

Glossary

anthropomorphic Described or thought of as having a human form or human attributes.

apprentice One who is learning a trade, art, or calling by practical experience under skilled workers.

citation A formal statement of the achievements of a person receiving an academic honor.

collage A creative work that resembles a composition in incorporating various materials or elements.

folktale A story that originates within a particular society or region to which people everywhere can relate.

genre A category of artistic composition, including literature, characterized by a particular form or style.

grandeur The quality or state of being grand or magnificent.

juvenile When referring to literature, being suitable for children or young people.

monotony Repetitious sameness of tone or sound.

outcast Someone who is either thrown out of a society or situation, or not allowed entrance in the first place.

parody A literary work in which the style of an author or work is closely imitated for comic effect or mockery.

protagonist The main character in a literary work.

pseudonym A fictitious name; when used by a writer, also called a pen name.

sentimental Resulting from feeling rather than reason or thought.

vulgar Used to describe something that is base, crude, or common.

whimsical Subject to unpredictable and fanciful behavior.

For More Information

Canadian Children's Book Centre
40 Orchard View Boulevard, Suite 217
Toronto, ON M4R 1B9
Canada
(416) 975-0010
Web site: http://www.bookcentre.ca
The Canadian Children's Book Centre is
a national organization dedicated to
promoting and supporting the creation
and consumption of Canadian books
for young readers. The organization
offers programs, publications, and
resources, and maintains an extensive
children's book collection by Canadian
authors.

Canadian Society of Children's
Authors, Illustrators and Performers
(CANSCAIP)
720 Bathurst Street, Suite 504
Toronto, ON M5S 2R4
Canada
(416) 515-1559
Web site: http://www.canscaip.org
CANSCAIP is a national arts service orga-
nization that supports and promotes
children's literature nationally through-
out Canada. The organization offers

newsletters, workshops, conferences, and mentorships for children's authors, illustrators, and performers.

Centre for Research in Young People's Texts and Cultures
3rd Floor Centennial Hall
University of Winnipeg
515 Portage Avenue
Winnipeg, MB R3B 2E9
Canada
(204) 786-7811
Web site: http://crytc.uwinnipeg.ca
The University of Winnipeg's Centre for Research in Young People's Texts and Cultures supports research and inquiry into literature and media for children and youth. The center publishes a journal and hosts visiting speakers and researchers on children's literary studies.

Children's Literature and Reading Special Interest Group
Washington State University
333 Cleveland Hall #310740
Pullman, WA 99164
(509) 335-6390
Web site: http://clrsig.org

Chartered by the International Reading Association, the Children's Literature and Reading Special Interest Group is dedicated to the development of high-quality children's literature. Each year, its Notable Books for a Global Society Committee selects and promotes the top twenty-five children's books that promote cross-cultural understanding and communication for young readers.

Children's Literature Association
1301 West 22nd Street, Suite 202
Oak Brook, IL 60523
(630) 571-4520
Web site: http://www.childlitassn.org
The Children's Literature Association is dedicated to criticism, scholarship, research, and education in the field of children's literature. The organization publishes two peer-reviewed journals on children's book studies and bestows awards for excellence in scholarship in children's literature.

Society of Children's Book Writers & Illustrators
8271 Beverly Boulevard

Los Angeles, CA 90048
(323) 782-1010
Web site: http://www.scbwi.org
The Society of Children's Book Writers &
Illustrators boasts membership spanning all fields in the process of producing
and promoting literature for children
and young adults. The society sponsors
biannual conferences, and regional chap-
ters provide comprehensive guides and
resources on writers of children's literature for readers and writers alike.

Web Sites

Due to the changing nature of Internet
links, Rosen Educational Services has developed an online list of Web sites related
to the subject of this book. This site is
updated regularly. Please use this link to
access the list:

http://www.rosenlinks.com/eafct/child

For Further Reading

Abrams, Dennis. *L. Frank Baum*. New York, NY: Chelsea House, 2010.

Bostrom, Kathleen L. *Winning Authors: Profiles of the Newbery Medalists*. Westport, CT: Libraries Unlimited, Inc., 2003.

Carroll, Pamela Sissi. *Sharon Creech*. Santa Barbara, CA: Greenwood, 2007.

Clarke, Nzingha. *Karen Hesse*. New York, NY: Rosen Publishing, 2005.

Cotter, Charis. *Born to Write: The Remarkable Lives of Six Famous Authors*. Toronto, Canada: Annick Press, Ltd., 2009.

Jones, Jen. *Judy Blume: Fearless Storyteller for Teens*. Berkeley Heights, NJ: Enslow Publishers , 2008.

Pascal, Janet. *Who Was Maurice Sendak?* New York, NY: Grosset & Dunlap, 2013.

Shavick, Andrea. *Roald Dahl: True Lives*. Oxford, England: Oxford University Press, 2009.

Silverthorne, Elizabeth. *Louisa May Alcott*. New York, NY: Chelsea House, 2011.

Index

215